Writing
for Radio

Writing for Radio

*How to write plays, features and
short stories that get you on air*

SHAUN MACLOUGHLIN

How To Books

Published by How To Books Ltd,
3 Newtec Place, Magdalen Road,
Oxford OX4 1RE, United Kingdom.
Tel: (01865) 793806. Fax: (01865) 248780.
email: info@howtobooks.co.uk
http://www.howtobooks.co.uk

First edition 1998
Second edition 2001

British Library Cataloguing in Publication Data.
A catalogue record for this book is available from
the British Library.

Cartoons by Mike Flanagan
Cover design by Shireen Nathoo Design
Cover image by PhotoDisc

Produced for How To Books by Deer Park Productions
Typeset by Kestrel Data, Exeter
Printed and bound by Cromwell Press Ltd, Trowbridge, Wiltshire

NOTE: The material contained in this book is set out in good
faith for general guidance and no liability can be accepted
for loss or expense incurred as a result of relying in particular
circumstances on statements made in the book. Laws and
regulations are complex and liable to change, and readers should
check the current position with the relevant authorities before
making personal arrangements.

Contents

Preface

AMDG was the dedication we put at the beginning of our school homework. It stands for *Ad Maiorem Dei Gloriam*: To The Greater Glory Of God. I have to thank the Jesuits for my love of literature and of the spoken word.

I should also like to dedicate this book to two women: my late, heroic mother, a one-time successful novelist and journalist, whose subsequent rejection slips could have papered the entire walls of the cottage where I was brought up; and Jane, my humorous, loyal wife who has put up with my vagaries for over 30 years. As our friend, Enyd Williams observed: 'Shaun is the Catholic and Jane is the Saint.'

I should also like to thank a multitude of writers, actors, composers, musicians, technicians, production assistants, students and fellow producers, who have helped to make my working life, as a radio drama producer, a joy and an inspiration. Many will be mentioned in these pages. In this second edition I should like to thank Tom Bennett, for his research into Internet drama sites, and the delightful Nikki Read, my editor at How To Books, for her encouragement. I am grateful to my friends – John Tydeman, ex-Head of BBC Radio Drama; Jonathan Smith, playwright, novelist and schoolmaster, and Badria Timimi, drama student – for their helpful and positive comments.

I should particularly like to honour the memory of the late Richard Imison, BBC Script Editor Radio Drama for over 20 years, whose perfectionism, creative intelligence and encouragement to writers helped radio drama to remain a considerable art form from the 1960s to the 1980s.

Finally I should like to thank the listeners, the audience without whom audio drama would not exist. It is not surprising that a high proportion of listeners and of radio playwrights are women. They are generally better listeners than men. I hope the reader will bear this in mind when from time to time I use the personal pronoun 'he'.

Shaun MacLoughlin

1

Understanding Why Radio is Different

COMPARING RADIO WITH OTHER MEDIA

Radio drama has been described variously as the 'Mind as Stage', 'The Theatre Between the Ears', 'The Theatre Where Anything That Can Be Imagined Can Happen' and 'The Auditorium of the Cranium'. The last phrase is ugly, but apt. In the early 1970s the Germans invented a stereophonic microphone that they called a *Kunstkopf* (literally an 'art-head'). It was constructed in the shape of a skull to capture sound as we actually receive it. BBC producers used to sit around with earphones, listening to recordings of a pin being dropped under a jet aircraft taking off at Tempelhof Airport, Berlin. The *Kunstkopf* bore a remarkable resemblance to the then Head of BBC Radio Drama, Martin Esslin.

However, radio drama is really about something more ancient and wonderful: 'In the beginning was the word'. It is primarily about the power and the beauty of the spoken word, that can convey to the human imagination anything of which it can conceive.

There is the mythical small boy who prefers radio to TV because the pictures are better and the colours more vivid. In *The Hitch-hiker's Guide To The Galaxy* 26 men can fit inside a sardine tin. In 1938 the comedian Arthur Askey declared: 'Radio is the only medium where a man can sit on a circular saw in outer space'. It is a medium for an audience with an active imagination. It is for listeners who like to participate and to contribute something from their rich and reflective experience of life. It is a medium which 'stimulates' the imagination, unlike TV which only 'satisfies' it.

Painting our own pictures

I should love to be a voyeur and see the pictures being formed inside the head of each listener to the following excerpt from Douglas Adams' marvellously inventive *The Hitch-hiker's Guide To The Galaxy*. We, each of us, bring something different to it.

Our picture of the characters speaking will gradually take shape and our picture of the man with five heads, of the wall, of the motion of Southend's sea front and of the colour of the sea, will vary from listener to listener. From the dialogue and the actors' performances and from our differing experience of life, we shall, each of us, conjure up our own characters.

FORD: Perhaps we'd better ask somebody what's going on. How about that man over there?

ARTHUR: The one with five heads creeping up the wall?

FORD: Er – yes (<u>Only a suspicion of a doubt in his voice</u>)

ARTHUR: Sir, excuse me, er – excuse me –

<u>F/X: WILD TRUMPETING AND BELLOWING LIKE AN ELEPHANT OR SOMETHING</u>

ARTHUR: You know, if this is Southend, there's something very odd about it.

FORD: You mean the way the sea stays steady as a rock and the buildings keep washing up and down? Yes, *I* thought that was odd –

I am going to give many illustrations from radio plays. I strongly recommend that you read them aloud to yourself or better still with your friends, fellow students or families. This will not only bring them alive for you, but will help you to hear the music, the pace and the rhythm of the language. It will help you to evoke the pictures. It will help your writing to be more beguiling. As a playwright you should attempt to be a reasonably good amateur actor. Reading aloud is also the only way to time a play and a stopwatch should be one of your first investments. Why not act out the previous passage – complete with sound effects?

TAPPING THE LISTENER'S IMAGINATION

When you are writing a radio play, remember two things:

1. That you are writing for **a single listener**. That single listener may hopefully be multiplied by hundreds of thousands, but you should write the play as if it takes place in the privacy of a single person's imagination.
2. Try to think of what can **only** happen in radio – or audio. In that way you will explore the medium at its most imaginative.

Although the structures of radio plays and of novels are quite different, they can act on the imagination in a similar manner. George Eliot said of the novel: 'No species of art is so free from rigid requirements. Like crystalline masses it may take any form, and yet be beautiful; we have only to pour in the right elements – genuine observation, humour and passion'. Henry James wrote: 'The novelist competes with his brother the painter in his attempt to render the look of things, the look that conveys their meanings, to catch the colour, the relief, the expression, the surface, the substance of the human spectacle.' I believe that what Eliot and James have to say applies even more to the creation of a radio play: a mysterious process, which is one of implicit connivance between playwright and listener. Of course the director, the actors and the technicians also have a hand. It is partly this team work that makes the creation of a radio play such a joy; a joy that can come as a reward to the normally solitary life of the playwright. Radio is very much a writer's medium.

Donald McWhinnie, in his excellent book *The Art Of Radio*, describes how the playwright stimulates the imagination: 'The world of visual detail which the listener creates is a world of limitless dimension; the images may be vivid, but they have no specific proportions; they exist in a world that is largely a dream world. The radio performance works on the mind in the same way as poetry does; it liberates and evokes.'

BEGINNING WITH AN IMAGE

In a radio play, language – sometimes assisted by sound effects, variety of acoustic space, music and comparative silence – has to accomplish far more than in any other medium. The language has to tell the story, reveal character and draw pictures in the theatre of the listener's mind.

Perhaps it is not surprising that many radio plays are first triggered by an image. For example the playwright Michael

Campbell saw a man with his shoes and trousers on, standing up to his knees in the sea, playing a violin. He never asked the man why he was doing this. Instead he used the image to start on a creative journey of his own and arrived at his own explanation in his play, *The Man Who Stood In The Sea*.

Another playwright, Juliet Ace, was fascinated by the story of Coco, the parrot, whose cage sat on the bar of the Hotel Commodore in Beirut, where journalists used to congregate. Her play takes place in 1982 immediately before the Israeli invasion of Lebanon. Coco used to amuse hard-bitten reporters by swearing in 22 different languages. Walid the barman was so jealous of the attention that the clients paid to Coco that, under cover of an Israeli bombardment, he shot the parrot. *Lobby Talk* was a 'pure' radio play, an aural experience that explored and extended the medium and that could not be expressed in any other form. The parrot is the narrator – until he is shot.

In performance this excerpt from the beginning lasted exactly three minutes. Again I suggest that you should try performing – and timing it – yourself. Be a parrot!

(THE GENERAL BACKGROUND NOISE IN THE HOTEL FOYER IS MUFFLED. WE ARE IN THE PARROT'S CAGE, WHICH IS COVERED BY A CLOTH.)

ANNOUNCER: 'Lobby Talk', a play dedicated to Coco the parrot by Juliet Ace and Vic Aicken, with Steve Hodson as Coco and Andrew Sachs as Walid.

COCO: When anyone asks why I am covered with a cloth at this time of day, Walid tells them I am getting on, and need an afternoon nap. The truth is, that whilst I could give him a good few years, my stamina, wit and untiring ability to communicate and delight, outstrip his meagre efforts. However, when he thinks to punish me, he does me a favour. Tea time at the Commodore is dead time. The faded Brits teeter in on high heels, bleating for toasted tea cakes, but settling for sticky pastry drenched in honey.

(SQUAWKS) But I am being remiss. My name is Coco. I might have preferred the dignity of Charles or Winston or Dwight . . . but in these difficult times, Coco is probably safer. My owner, a journalist whose name does not spring immediately to mind, left me here some years ago. Fouad, the Manager, could see that the ladies and gentlemen of the press, far from home and family, would appreciate someone who could speak to them in their own language and be sympathetic in their darker moments. So here I am. (SQUAWKS TWICE) I rank pretty high in parrot terms. I may not match particular parrots who appear in novels of magical realism . . . But – and this is important – I exist. I am internationally famous and I have learnt to speak more languages than any other parrot I have heard of. You must understand however that I cannot separate one language from another . . . I do not have that facility. Therefore I hear all languages as one. A language whose vocabulary extends into millions of words. More complex than Esperanto and without accent. What I hear, you will hear.

(THE CLOTH IS WHIPPED OFF THE CAGE. THE HOTEL SOUNDS ARE AUGMENTED TO PROPER PITCH)

WALID: OK. Wake up. But behave yourself. One word out of place, I might shut you up for good.

COCO: (INTERNAL VOICE) Boring little man. (ALOUD. SQUAWKS) Gimme a Scotch.

WALID: Shut up.

COCO: Gimme a Scotch. A large one you fool.

WALID: (HIGH PITCHED) Shut up! Shut up!

(COCO WHISTLES THE FIRST COUPLE OF BARS OF THE MARSEILLAISE HITTING A FINAL WRONG NOTE)

WALID: (OFF) One day he'll open his mouth once too often.

COCO: (INTERNAL VOICE) And so will he.

The author elegantly solves the problem of the characters speaking many different languages. Also you will notice how she builds up and gradually pieces together both the narrative and the pictures. In radio the unfolding of the story and the encouragement of the listeners to create pictures in their minds are crucially connected.

CONSIDERING SHAKESPEARE AND OTHER AUDIO PLAYWRIGHTS

Shakespeare, writing 300 years before the invention of the medium, was, paradoxically, an excellent radio playwright. His language is full of pictures: of descriptions of scenery, of dress and of characters. The audience (from the Latin *audire*: to hear) used to go to the Globe Theatre not to 'see' but to 'hear' a play. There was virtually no scenery, just costume and a few props. The groundlings and the gallery were encouraged to create the scenery in their heads.

In the 20th century there are hardly any major playwrights who have not learnt, developed and/or mastered their art in radio before moving on to theatre, film and TV. Samuel Beckett, Robert Bolt, Caryl Churchill, Ethan Coen, Anthony Minghella, Arthur Miller, John Mortimer, Clifford Odets, Harold Pinter, Tom Stoppard, Dylan Thomas, Sue Townsend and Fay Weldon are just a few names that spring to mind; and most of them have frequently revisited radio, their first love.

In radio they learnt how the spoken word, almost alone, can with skill and economy accomplish everything. It is in radio that they have come nearer to fulfilling three of my favourite precepts: 'Industry, intelligence and imagination' (Gwen Ffrancon Davies), 'True, clear and interesting' (Prunella Scales) and 'Faith, hope and clarity' (Dorothy Reynolds).

UNDERSTANDING WHAT MAKES A GOOD RADIO PLAY

A little history

In radio you can have a cast of thousands and you can span centuries and continents. You can make the equivalent of a film like *Titanic* for a thousandth of the cost. You can also enter the recesses of a person's mind. It can be the most intimate of media. It is a wonderfully liberating medium, yet the craft of writing a radio play is one of the hardest to master.

But what essentially makes a *good* radio play? In order to gain an insight into this, I am going to give you a little history. Most of the early radio plays in the 1920s were adaptations of stage plays. As Cecil Lewis said in 1923:

> So far, we have largely contented ourselves (I think wisely) with Shakespeare, whose amazing beauty lies almost entirely in the spoken word as a means of presenting character and situation. No better plays for broadcasting could have been written.

One of the first plays written specifically for Radio was *Danger* by the novelist Richard Hughes. He wrote it in 1923 in 24 hours to fill a gap in the schedules. In an article in the *Radio Times* he advised:

> The scene of the play is laid in a mine, and to help the atmosphere, it is suggested that listeners might well sit in darkness to correspond with the play's setting.

The play began with the speech: 'The lights have gone out'. It could only work on radio. The listener was invited to identify with a group of trapped miners. Radio was beginning already to come to terms with a mass, as opposed to a West End, audience. There was one exception: the article advised parents not to allow their children to listen, lest they be frightened.

Audience response was enthusiastic. Over a thousand letters and postcards arrived at the BBC, including one from the leading actress Ellen Terry:

> No greater performance have I ever heard, which has produced such a thrill on an unseen audience, another step forward has been taken by the BBC.

Shortly afterwards, the blind writer R C Scriven wrote a play about an eye operation called *The Single Taper*. From the start writers were thinking, 'What makes a radio play different from other plays?'

The history of radio drama and, for a brief period when it nearly became a major art form, the history of television drama can both be enlightening to the aspiring radio writer.

Major art forms
In television 30 years ago four or five new plays by new or major playwrights were broadcast every week. In 1965 *Cathy Come Home* by Jeremy Sandford and *A Breach In The Wall*, a new play about a miracle at Canterbury by Ray Lawler, attracted audiences of twelve million and that was when only about half the population of the United Kingdom had access to television. In the North of England, men were leaving the pubs at ten past nine (in those days the news lasted only 15 minutes) to be home for BBC's *The Wednesday Play*. It is revealing to compare these figures to the audience, pro rata, for *EastEnders*. It might have been better, both artistically and commercially, if television had remained writer-, rather than management-, led. In the 1990s, under John Birt's stewardship, radio drama showed signs of aping television's mistakes, but as we go to press is thankfully appearing to recover.

In his preface to a collection of Best Radio Plays for 1988, Richard Imison wrote:

> Taken on their own the statistics of radio drama as an active part of British cultural life between 1978 and 1988 are really rather impressive . . . [There are] some three and a half thousand original radio plays broadcast by the BBC. These plays had been commissioned for the most part from among the hundred thousand completed scripts and synopses submitted to the Radio Drama department during this period. More than five thousand writers were regularly involved in writing radio plays and many more occasionally gave the medium a try. All these figures are dwarfed however by the number of times individual listeners switched on a radio play in the course of the past ten years: a prodigious ten billion.

Radio drama has a magnificent past and hopefully a bright future in the form perhaps not of radio, but of 'sound' or 'audio' drama on cassette and on the Internet. Let us hope that the BBC will continue to maintain and further its role of guardian of the great British cultural tradition of radio drama.

It is as a lover of the medium from my first childhood memories and as a script editor and producer of some 30 years' experience that I am writing this book. I invite you to share the firm and fervent hope that audio drama is an art form that still has far to go.

You have no doubt bought this book because you are interested in writing and selling an audio play, feature or short story. Now let us get down to practicalities.

2

Starting a Radio Play

GETTING STARTED

Establishing a routine and ritual

As a writer you will have to acquire discipline. You may need to learn to impose regular hours and rituals upon yourself. You should try and discover the right pattern: one you will stick to and which yields the best results.

Fay Weldon, one of the busiest and most productive writers I know, says that the only time to write is early in the morning; but that one must sharpen one's pencils and have one's paper ready or prepare one's computer the night before. In that way one will have as few distractions as possible and hopefully the muse will not depart before one gets down to work. She goes on to say that the same rules apply as used to apply to writing a school essay. Some people will prepare very well. Others will do it in a desperate last minute rush. She could not resist adding: 'Often the harder you try, the worse marks you will get'.

Peter Tinniswood, author of numerous stylish and highly original radio plays, gets up every day at about 6.30 and is at his computer by 8. He then works till 11.30 when he goes shopping and pays a short visit to a pub, where in the summer he can see a bit of the test match. Then back to a light lunch and on with work until about 4.30 pm when he will do any further chores required and pay a second brief visit to the pub, often with a mate like myself. Thus on his writing days he is working concentratedly for about six hours.

Mike Walker, author of hundreds of radio plays and creative features, finds starting a new project the hardest challenge. So he works himself in, spends only 10 minutes on the first day and then maybe half an hour on the second. On the third day he gets down to his regular routine of starting when his wife leaves to teach at 8.30 in the morning and works through to lunch. He often takes an oxygen inducing, weight reducing cycle ride in the early after-noon, before working through again from 4.30–6.30. If he has a deadline he will work straight through to bedtime without a break.

Tina Pepler, one of the most original young playwrights in the country, spends a long preparation period, in which she makes hundreds of notes on cards. She then creates or discovers the shape of her play from her arrangement of the cards, like completing a jig-saw puzzle. The actual writing of the play comes last and is a very fast and concentrated process.

Colin Haydn Evans, author of radio plays on a remarkable diversity of subjects and in an equally remarkable diversity of styles, is highly disciplined; though as he says himself, 'perhaps not in a formal way'. When he has a play commissioned he calculates precisely how long it will take him to write, on the assumption that he will complete three minutes of play a day. (His first draft is composed entirely of dialogue, with no directions or effects.) Thus a 60 minute play will take 20 working days. Since, he says, this target is well under his usual average output he can be confident that he will always meet the deadline.

Peter Terson will sit in cafés sketching people and out of these characters and situations his plays will grow and evolve. His play scripts are wonderfully picturesque. At one time he wrote and illustrated them on wall paper. We used to have to crawl around the office floor to read them and to enjoy the pictures. How to get a producer down on his knees!

I do not believe Hilaire Belloc wrote any plays, but when asked why he kept on writing, at least 140 books, he replied, 'To keep my children in jewellery and caviar'. Nick McCarty simply puts the notice 'Mortgage!' in front of him on the desk.

Each writer, by trial and error, must find their own method. If you work to a disciplined pattern a great deal of thought and creativity will happen during your 'fallow' periods. I have been lucky enough to write this book mostly during short breaks between other projects, beside the sea in Vietnam and Cambodia. I find that most of my memories and ideas come to me, after about six hours at my laptop, when eating alone or when swimming; or in England, when cycling or walking. Also one will quite often wake up in the night with a new idea or the solution to a problem. Be sure to have a notebook and pen handy to jot it down.

As a Jewish writer friend of mine says, 'Miracles are damned carefully prepared!'

GRABBING THE AUDIENCE

The beginning of the play

BBC Radio 4's commissioning brief for the 45-minute Afternoon Play slot states that programmes should have 'clear and beguiling openings and use their opening credits to set up the play and make listening as easy as possible'.

In radio you do not have a *captive* audience, who have paid for a seat, who might be embarrassed to leave and who will therefore give the play a chance to develop. On TV and more so on radio the audience can very quickly switch off, first mentally and then physically. As Sidney Newman, the charismatic and forthright Head of BBC TV Drama in the 1960s, said: 'Catch them by the goolies as they get up to switch the set off and you've got them for half an hour'. Radio is a less sensational, but potentially a more beguiling medium than television. Having made the unusual career move from TV to radio, I think I am entitled to make this claim!

The switch off button is never far away. As a writer you probably have about a minute, two at the outside, to engage your listener. However wonderful the rest of the play, if your beginning does not captivate the listeners, they will never stay to be enchanted.

Examples of beginnings

Let's look at the beginning of a famous radio play, first broadcast in 1957:

ANNOUNCER: This is the BBC Third Programme. We present a play by Giles Cooper entitled, 'The Disagreeable Oyster'.

BUNDY: You can say that again.

ANNOUNCER: 'The Disagreeable Oyster'.

BUNDY: They do disagree with me, but how was I to know when I stood on the steps of the Rosedene Family and Commercial Hotel, thinking that the world was my oyster that –

BUNDY MINOR:	Begin at the beginning.
BUNDY:	And the beginning is at twelve o'clock on a Saturday morning in my office at Craddock's Calculators Ltd.

It is a period piece, but no less entertaining for that. It is about a very ordinary person in a very ordinary situation and yet because the story is presented in a stylish and amusing way, one wants to listen on. This beginning conveys necessary information without spelling it out in an obvious, boring or clumsy way. It also begins to establish the conventions that Bundy, the central character, can step outside the action of the play and talk to the announcer, and that Bundy is divided into two parts, the more thoughtful being Bundy Minor.

Let's look at the beginning of a more recent play, and see how much information the playwright divulges in an oblique and entertaining manner.

(MUSIC: OLD RECORDING OF THE SONG 'LOVE IS THE SWEETEST THING')

ANNOUNCER: 'Hard of Hearing' by Colin Haydn Evans.

(FADE MUSIC. SFX OF TWO PEOPLE EATING BREAKFAST).

JUNE:	I was reading the other day of this man who used to talk to hedgehogs. The only problem he said was that he never knew the meaning of what he said to them.

(BRIAN SIGHS)

JUNE:	Lyme Regis. I think he lived in Lyme Regis.
BRIAN:	Er-hum.
JUNE:	He did not know the meaning of what he said to them.

(PAUSE)

BRIAN:	June, are you trying to say something?
JUNE:	Yes.
BRIAN:	Over breakfast?
JUNE:	It's Saturday, Brian.
BRIAN:	Ruddy Mecca, if you ask me. Light at the end of the week's tunnel.
JUNE:	Didn't Maureen used to have a residential caravan near there? It's in Dorset isn't it, Lyme Regis? They used to spend the second half of September in it.

(BRIAN SIGHS AGAIN)

JUNE:	He went on to say that the principle could be equally well applied to the Colorado Beetle. Talking to them, I mean. He felt it might be good news for potato farmers.
BRIAN:	Toast.
JUNE:	(TO HERSELF) He said grazing her eyes with his.
BRIAN:	If you want any more there won't be enough.

(SFX: SHE PUTS ANOTHER SLICE INTO TOASTER)

JUNE:	(ALOUD) I like people who do silly things. I think it's comforting. (TO HERSELF) If you don't say something soon you page three moron you're going to get this piece of cremated bread right up your pre-soaked shirt. Fancy that do you? (ALOUD) What Love?

This is the beginning of a marvellous comedy, in which Brian devotes Saturday morning to attempting to mend the washing machine and spends half the play with his head stuck in it – an interesting acoustic. (He has programmed the door to remain open while the drum revolves and his tie gets caught round it). Not unlike *The Disagreeable Oyster*, the play starts in an everyday, conventional setting with ordinary people, though the listener senses that an intriguing story is about to unfold. It also establishes one character's inner voice, that the other character cannot hear.

In talking to aspiring radio playwrights, who ask me what I am looking for, I often say: 'Please, surprise me. Please give me something I have never encountered before.' But I also say, 'If you can start a play with ordinary people in an ordinary setting, with whom many listeners will identify, then if you can make that really entertaining and different, I shall be delighted.'

Let's look at the beginning of a play that could hardly be more different. *Babylon Has Fallen*, by John Fletcher, has a much less conventional setting – that of a Victorian tropical island where Augustus Hare, an old Etonian roué with a Malaysian harem, and David Worth, a non-conformist evangelist with a band of pious disciples, confront one another. The writer, who is something of a visionary, has allowed his imagination free rein. He also wrote a stage version of the play, in which, at the beginning, the characters were brought on and introduced to the audience. This he felt would not be so engaging in the radio version, which starts as follows:

(HIGHLY DRAMATIC, VICTORIAN ORGAN MUSIC)

DAVID: One Morning the Lord God Ravished I. As I did sit at Sunday service, the sun full in the aisle, playing a voluntary upon the organ, a flare of raw light did hit my body, burnt so strong, I could see every bone glowing within my hands. While all about I the world fell dark and dead. And as He did ravish I, the Lord God implanted within I the seed of wisdom. 'Go, David Worth,' He said, 'leave your Babylonian captivity here in Bristol. Seek out a place unsullied by human habitation and there build for me the Temple of the new Jerusalem.'

(FADE ORGAN MUSIC)

> From that moment there has been no distraction in my life. At night I studied the holy texts of Revelation, seeking to understand the sacred principles of Divine Geometry. Upon old ocean charts I found an island, the Keeling Coco Island, lying deep in the wastes of the Great Southern Ocean. Myself, all my companions, my wife and children, my faithful servant Elisha all scrimped and saved, husbanded our scarce resources, until one day last Spring after many hardships, us set sail from our native Bristol, down the Gorge of Avon and out upon the broad ocean, committing ourselves to the perilous deep.

(BRING UP AND SWELL SAILING SHIP CUTTING THROUGH HEAVY SEAS AND INTO THE NEXT SCENE)

Here we have a larger than life character in a relatively unusual situation. However, what this beginning has in common with the two earlier examples is that it is starting to tell a story. If these beginnings have done their job properly for you, as they have for me, I am intrigued, even compelled, to listen on, to know what is going to happen next. Incidentally, the fading of the organ music subtly directs the listener away from the chapel and inside David's head, rather as one might track into close-up on film.

KNOWING WHERE TO START YOUR PLAY

The beginning is vital. As a script editor and drama director for over 30 years, I must have commented upon tens of thousands of scripts. One of the questions I most frequently ask promising writers is, 'Do you think you have begun your play in the right place?' This is because I have got into the habit of making a note of where I first became involved and really wanted to know what was going to happen next.

Page 27 in a 60-page script sticks in my mind. This perhaps, on average, is the point, when I say to myself, particularly where a promising new writer is concerned: 'Ah, this is interesting, at last. This is what the play is about. This is where the story really begins. This is why you are writing the play.' Very often up to this point you, the aspiring writer, may have been writing yourself into the play, discovering what it is about. You have gone through the necessary process of producing a first draft. But I must warn you that very probably the script is not yet ready to submit to a busy script editor or producer, who might well reject it out of hand.

I did not work with David Zane Mairowitz on his play *Dictator Gal* and do not know whether this was his original opening. But it is certainly gripping:

(FEEBLE BREATHING OF PATIENT. ELECTROCARDIOGRAM CONNECTED TO ELECTRONIC STETHOSCOPE. HEARTBEAT AUDIBLE: SLOW, IRREGULAR. REGULAR HUM OF HOSPITAL MACHINERY ESTABLISHES. DOOR QUIETLY CLOSED. QUIET FOOTSTEPS. DOCTOR HUMS 'STRANGER IN PARADISE'. CURTAIN FOLDED BACK. PATIENT BREATHING.)

DOCTOR: (Murmuring to himself: writing on chart) Pressure. 40 over 10; pulse – 30 – 30? Not worth it. Bon Voyage Mr – Mr – er – Flannigan –.

(PLUG PULLED. MACHINERY COMES TO A NOISY DEFINITIVE STOP. GURGLING NOISE FROM PATIENT BECOMES LOUDER. BODY MOVEMENT UNDER SHEETS. GASPING. LONG DEATH THROES.)

(*Naturally*) Shh! You'll wake the other patients.

(DOCTOR LEAVES ROOM STILL HUMMING 'STRANGER IN PARADISE'. THE PATIENT GIVES A FINAL GASP. CONTINUOUS BLEEP OF LIFE SUPPORT SYSTEM INDICATES THAT PATIENT'S HEART HAS STOPPED)

Would you want to listen on?

WRITING FOR A SOPHISTICATED AUDIENCE

Tina Pepler's *Easy Traumas* was written for a sophisticated Radio 3 audience, who are probably prepared to devote more concentration to listening than a Radio 4 Afternoon Play audience, who may be distracted by housework, driving or small children. It is not so much that the people who listen to drama on Radios 2, 3 and 4 are different. In fact audience research indicates that they are probably the same people, but that they are listening in different circumstances.

Easy Traumas concerns an angelic agency that helps you to cope with the worst crises in your life: death, divorce, house-moving, loss of a banana milk-shake, etc; though the listener will only learn this as the play develops.

ANNOUNCER: Introducing the Easy Traumas Agency. Take it away Castor Sugar.

CASTOR SUGAR: Hi!

ANNOUNCER: And Pollux.

POLLUX: Hello there.

   (SNAFFLE DRUM)

ANNOUNCER: Deborah Makepeace plays Castor Sugar, Steve Hodson plays Pollux, Christian Rodska plays Barny and Liz Goulding plays Wilma in Easy Traumas by Tina Pepler.

POLLUX: Let go into the healing power of hatred.

CASTOR SUGAR: Get smart about falling apart.

POLLUX: Get wise to your own demise.

CASTOR SUGAR: We work fast from the outside in. No introspection.

POLLUX: Don't think. .

CASTOR SUGAR: Don't wonder about what went wrong.

POLLUX: Whatever you do don't think.

CASTOR SUGAR: Just do it.

POLLUX: Your thoughts will catch up with your instincts.

CASTOR SUGAR: Easy Traumas.

POLLUX: Bizarre, yes. Cruel, perhaps. Indifferent, almost certainly. But we know what we are saying.

CASTOR SUGAR: Are we shallow?

POLLUX: Are we cruel?

CASTOR SUGAR: You bet your bottom we are.

POLLUX: But we're very good communicators.

CASTOR SUGAR: You need us.

POLLUX: Barnie.

CASTOR SUGAR: You may not know it, but you need us.

(START TO FADE DRUM AND SPEECH)

POLLUX: Let go.

CASTOR SUGAR: Let go.

POLLUX: Let go.

As did Giles Cooper in *The Disagreeable Oyster*, so Tina Pepler has the announcer enter the play to interact with the characters.

Fay Weldon has commented wryly and wittily on most aspects

of contemporary life, so why not on the writing and producing of a radio play? Here is the beginning of *The Hole In The Top Of The World*, a BBC/Los Angeles Theatre Works co-production, starring Walter Matthau. Fay Weldon imagines that Matt, the central character, is making a radio play about his life story:

(THE SOUND OF WHISTLING ANTARCTIC WINDS. IT DIES AS MATT SPEAKS. MATT IS 60'ISH, EDUCATED, CHARMING, DANGEROUS, TRANSATLANTIC. HE'S BEEN EVERYWHERE, DONE EVERYTHING.)

MATT: Did you get that, radio freaks? That wasn't the desert winds over the High Sierra. That was the winds whistling in Antarctica. What you're hearing is the icy bit at the bottom of the world. Though, as they tell you in Australia, since there's no up and down in space, it's as reasonable to call it the top as the bottom. That way the Australians can get to be not down under but on top. If that suits them, that's okay by me. I'm not in the business of making anyone feel bad. All I ever wanted to do was move the world on a bit; understand the material universe. Why are scientists so unpopular? Is there something wrong with harnessing the power of the sun, curing melanoma? You people out there are ungrateful. I won't say stupid – you'd switch off. And then I'd have wasted good money on this sound studio, hiring these airwaves.

I know I called you freaks, but don't take it too hard: face it, you're listening to the radio, not watching TV, and that makes you the last of the listeners; all you want is someone's voice to fill the space between your ears. What you want is what God never gave us. A story with a beginning, a middle, and an end; a point and a purpose. Some kind of pattern in amongst the chaos. All I ever wanted, or worked for. Now they're all at it. Catastrophe Theory, Fractals. My generation paved the way: and is anyone grateful? No. Listen again.

(SX. WIND. ADD SEAGULLS)

That fooled you. Seagulls signify a coast. A coastline in Antarctica? Well okay.

(ADD HOOTING OWLS)

Okay, make that night. The coast of Antarctica at night.

(ADD TRAFFIC SOUNDS)

A little town at night on the coast of Antarctica.

(ADD POLICE SIRENS)

A big town at night on some cliff on Antarctica.

(FADE POLICE SIRENS. ADD TOLLING OF CHURCH BELLS)

A churchyard? No – here the mind boggles. That's what I had in mind for you, the boggling of the mind. Overload. Even if I told you that was a high wind in Jamaica –

(LOSE CHURCH BELLS. INTRODUCE WIND PLUS THE BANANA BOAT SONG)

you'd still have trouble. So forget it. Let's have some silence.

(SILENCE. HOLD IT)

Silence is frightening. Nothingness.

Silence is certainly powerful. Donald McWhinnie in 1959 in *The Art of Radio* quotes a woman, a devotee of the 'telly', who referred to the radio as the 'silent'. McWhinnie wrote that she had stumbled on a truth: 'paradoxically there is silence at the heart of the radio experience, it might almost be unspoken communication between writer and listener'. Also silence is the frame within which a radio play takes place.

SETTING THE SCENE AND THE ATMOSPHERE

I am going to end this chapter with an excerpt from one of the most enchanting plays it has been my privilege to work on. Unlike the other examples it is not from an original play. It is a dramatisation of a Russian novel. Dramatisation is not easy and I would never encourage an aspiring writer to attempt to adapt a novel and still less a TV or screenplay, until they have had at least two or three original plays produced for radio.

(THE SEVENTH SYMPHONY OF THEODORAKIS ESTABLISHES ITSELF THEN PLAYS VERY GENTLY BEHIND THE FOLLOWING)

LEONID: It is twenty five years since I gave my word to the old lady, Sarma. What happened, happened in the time of my childhood. It has probably happened to lots of children, who are perhaps afraid of not being believed. So they kept silent.

(MUSIC FADES)

They at least will believe me.

(THE MUSIC GENTLY RE-EMERGES)

At this point I must issue a warning. I would not waste your time on some harmless, if amusing little fairy tale. You may find it difficult, but I beg you to try to break through the barrier of disbelief. I have learnt, you see, that the truth, which exists within us, is immensely greater than the truth, which is revealed to us in the form of rules and laws in this world of ours.

(WE STAY WITH THE MUSIC FOR A MOMENT AND THEN, GENTLY AT FIRST, THE SOUND OF A DISTANT STEAM TRAIN EMERGES FROM WITHIN IT).

A miracle is something that occurs in spite of and contrary to everything. According to the rules it does not happen. Consequently when a miracle does take place, it does so in defiance of the rules.

You've never experienced a miracle? Not even a trifling, little miracle? I can help. Listen. No need to go to the ends of the earth. All you need is to go to the town of Irkutsk, board the Irkutsk to Slyudyanka train and sit on the left hand side of the carriage, facing forward.

(TRAIN WHISTLES. MAINTAIN STEAM TRAIN AND MUSIC IN BACKGROUND)

ANNOUNCER: 'The Year of Miracle and Grief' by Leonid Borodin, dramatised by Nick McCarty. Leonid Borodin was born in 1938 on the shores of Lake Baikal. Since 1966 he has been imprisoned twice for his Orthodox Christian beliefs. He was finally released in 1987. We present Steve Hodson as Leonid in 'The Year of Miracle and Grief'.

(WE MIX TO INTERIOR OF TRAIN CARRIAGE)

YOUNG LEONID: Will it be much longer, Papa?

FATHER: Not much longer, Leonid. Go to sleep, boy.

And so, the scene and the atmosphere are set and now the play proper can begin. Here the writer has promised to take us on a journey into and out of childhood, to tell us a story, to share a vision and to reveal a mystery. You can hardly do better than that.

You will note that the directions in this excerpt identify the music. In fact Nick McCarty talked to me (the director) about how important the music would be in establishing and sustaining an atmosphere of power and mystery. He suggested the Greek composer Theodorakis. Then he and I did a lot of listening, while acting out and timing some of the narrative passages, and seeing how we could engineer music and language to blend effectively together.

I always encourage the writer to do this as much as possible at an early stage. The writer is responsible not just for the language, but for the entire sound track: sound effects, music, acoustic and silence as well. As director I want to know everything that the writer hears in his head. I want all these elements to be in the script as part of the overall composition, just as I would want all the instrumental parts to be there, if I were conducting an orchestra.

You will note that several of the examples of beginnings of plays that I have given consist of a single voice narrative, mostly by a central character talking in the first person. A few years ago the narrator rather went out of fashion, but now appears to be coming back. The power and beauty of the single human voice, well produced and acted, can provide a compelling and cajoling way into a play. If kept fairly short, the contrast of 'opening up' from this overture into a scene in a concrete place, with more than one voice, can both fulfil a promise and be quite arresting. It can be the second movement of your symphony.

We shall say more about how to continue a play in the next chapter.

3

Structuring a Radio Play

STARTING AT THE END

In the last chapter we looked at how to begin a play. In order to arrive at an overall structure or design, at a shape that will continuously captivate the listener, it would not be a bad idea at this stage to think about the ending.

'In my beginning is my end' (T S Eliot's *Four Quartets*) contains an important truth for dramatists. Perhaps, more appositely, this should be reversed: 'In my end is my beginning'. Some dramatists may have to complete the first draft to discover the meaning of where they are starting from. They may end up like the Irishman, who, when asked how to get to Castlebar, replied, 'If I wanted to get to Castlebar, I wouldn't start from here in the first place'.

Some writers have no idea at all, when they start, either what they want to say or where the characters are leading them. The process of writing itself will be a journey of discovery.

Peter Tinniswood says that if he knows the end of the play when he is a quarter of the way in, he knows it is going to work. If he doesn't, he may still solve the ending by going back to the beginning and writing that in a different way.

We looked at the beginning of Colin Haydn Evans' play *Hard Of Hearing* in the last chapter and will look at the ending of it later in this chapter. He rarely knows how a play is going to end, when he starts it. For him the ending is in a state of constant flux and can change several times. Knowing the conclusion beforehand would be like the tail wagging the dog. He would always feel that he had to move down a certain road in a precise way to arrive at a set destination.

He goes on to say that the characters themselves dictate most of what will take place. Some will flatly refuse certain endings – others demand them. If he tries to impose a false conclusion (false that is in terms of the *real* theme) they revolt by withholding meaningful dialogue; resorting solely to cliché. He can literally then no longer 'write' them. Only when he lets them have their heads again will they resume speaking to him.

Thus, Haydn Evans claims, when writers claim that characters come 'alive' it is no exaggeration. Writing, he says, is not the lonely business it is popularly thought to be. Everyday the writer walks into a room full of people and yesterday's silent, often intriguing conversations reopen. He says 'I am not sure this is entirely healthy – but happen it does! There are lines in my plays which I quite genuinely feel have nothing at all to do with me. It was the characters solely. All I did was listen'.

Other writers will have a clear purpose and a definite ending in mind from the start. There are no absolutes about this. In fact one of the joys of working on and listening to really good radio plays is to appreciate how different is the approach of each writer.

In any case I have put this chapter next, because I think it a good idea to be wrestling with the problem of structure at an early stage in the process of writing a play. If the first draft has a structure which is attractive to the listener, then one may be on one's way to writing a hugely popular play.

If you have a beginning and an end in mind, it may be easier to plan the richness and variety of the journey in between. On the other hand you may lose something of the spontaneity of discovery. I am reminded of Jean Luc Godard, the French film director, who, when asked whether he thought his plays should have a beginning, a middle and an end, replied in his charming French accent, 'Yes definitely, but not necessarily in that order'.

GIVING SHAPE

Apply your mind to the end of the play as you might to the end of a pilgrimage, to give shape and meaning to your journey, to your narrative. It does not matter if the end changes radically in the course of writing the play. This will probably be because you have found ways of improving it. However, it can be a good idea to start with a shape to give yourself an even better shape.

Why not ask yourself, 'Why am I writing this play?', 'What do I want to say?', 'What thoughts and feelings do I want to leave the listener with at the end of the play?'

It may be helpful to examine the endings of two of the plays, whose beginnings we examined in the last chapter. First *The Year of Miracle and Grief*. The novel, of course, already has an ending. Thus, although the beginning and the ending of the dramatisation may not be exactly the same as in the novel, you will have a good idea as to where you are aiming. A note of explanation: Ri has been young Leonid's first love.

LEONID: We were to move again to another school in Siberia. I wanted to say good bye to Ri at the end of the term

(GENTLE STEAMING OF STATIONARY TRAIN)

RI: I have to go Leon

YOUNG LEONID: Yes. I – I will always remember you Rienka.

(FOOTSTEPS AND DISTANT ECHOING HOOT OF ENGINE)

LEONID: She climbed up the step into the carriage and I never again saw the girl from Dead Man's Crag

(TRAIN GENTLY DEPARTS. FADE TO SILENCE)

YOUNG LEONID: Vayerka gave me his three-bladed penknife and Svetka gave me a book and I said good-bye to them.

LEONID: And good-bye to Lake Baikal. I remembered Ri holding a yellow snow-drop in her hand on the first day of the thaw.

(GENTLE STEAMING AGAIN)

                  And then we too got into the train and that parting was without real pain. A childhood remains a childhood.

(THE STEAM TRAIN STARTS TO DEPART)

                  My memories of what had happened on the shores of Lake Baikal gradually blurred and, only if I find myself alone on a moonlit night, will the crescent of the new moon cause me to return to the sadness of the past. Possibly all my past has been nothing more than a preparation for my return.

(THE TRAIN BEGINS TO SPEED UP. DISTANT HOOT)

I feel sure that one day I shall go to Irkutsk,

(THE THEME MUSIC FROM THEODOKARIS STARTS VERY GENTLY)

board a train to Slyudyanka, and sit on the left hand side of the carriage. Then when the break in the mountains unveils the blue water and the brown crags, I shall discover for myself the essence of what is called the meaning of life. A miracle? Oh Yes!

(SWELL MUSIC AND TRAIN AND THEN INTO CLOSING CREDITS)

If you refer back to the beginning, you will see the connection with the end and perhaps, without reading the novel or listening to the play, you could have a go at writing the journey in between. You will probably not sell the result, but it could be an interesting exercise.

Now that we know something of the process by which he arrived there, let us have a look at the ending of Colin Haydn Evans' *Hard Of Hearing*. It was a half hour play and for almost half of it Brian's head is stuck in the washing machine with his tie caught in the works. He goes on and on criticising June, until eventually she flips and turns on the machine. He wakes up in hospital having suffered concussion and a broken nose. At this point we begin to hear his inner thoughts for the first time. Perhaps, unlike his wife, he has up to now, for many years, suppressed his thoughts. The play ends with a kind of reconciliation and with June and Brian going to bed together at three o'clock in the afternoon:

BRIAN: (TO HIMSELF) Being angry is being recognised. June got the brunt of it, I suppose. Kept asking, 'Why!?'

Never saw that if I knew why, I'd never have been like that in the first place.

JUNE: (ALOUD, ON ECHO FROM PAST) How do you mean: 'thinking of me'?

BRIAN: (TO HIMSELF) That's how the fondness goes, I suppose. Nobody keeping their lives to themselves. Trying to make others do their living for them. Turning marriage into an encounter group and sex into a bloody space launch. (PAUSE) The snag is, I think, when you get it right, you never really know. That leaves the door open for someone to tell you it isn't. That way you end up with your head in a washing machine. Brainwashing!

JUNE: (TO HERSELF) And why will I stay? They say people grow lonely as they get older. Then they need to turn to someone. Forty-four's not that old really. You never know, he may turn out quite nicely in the end.

BRIAN: (TO HIMSELF) I never wanted to be understood. Just liked.

JUNE: (TO HERSELF) Marriage isn't a miracle after all. It's just two people looking for one, which makes it twice as hard to find.

(SHE STIRS IN BED AND SIGHS)

JUNE: (ALOUD) There's still time before tea, Brian.

BRIAN: What? Oh yeah.

(MUSIC: 'LOVE IS THE SWEETEST THING'.

The shape of the play and the comedy give the author the opportunity to share with us in some depth his thoughts on the nature of marriage. Notice that in a sense the ending of this play is contained in, or at least promised by, the beginning.

PLANNING THE STRUCTURE IN BETWEEN

So how do you get from the beginning to the end? Here are a few pointers.

1. Make sure that your listener always wants to know what is going to happen next.

2. Construct your play like a symphony, with different movements, paces and styles to beguile and enchant the ear.

3. Prune well for healthy growth. A German dramatist once said that nine tenths of a writer's work is cutting.

Richard Imison probably read more radio scripts than anybody else in history. He said that from flicking through a script, just looking at the shape of its layout on a succession of pages, he could get an idea of how good the play was going to be. I was sceptical at first, but grew to agree with him. He was talking about what I call the match between music and meaning. The variety of pace, texture, acoustic of a play both from one scene to another and within each scene is important. Such contrasts can simultaneously beguile the ear and emphasise the message.

One of the many qualities that make Shakespeare a good radio writer was his instinctive realisation of this. He will frequently cut back and forth between poetry and prose, between soliloquy and dialogue, between the interior of a man's mind and a group of characters on a battlefield or in the depths of a wood; on a blasted heath or in an orchard; in a grand hall or a dungeon. Each change of acoustic, texture and pace will induce us to prick up our ears.

Similarities with a symphony

Another way to look at the structure of a radio play is to think of it as a musical composition. What is it about a great symphony that enthrals one? There could be as many answers as there are appreciative listeners. It could be the sheer beauty, the power, the amazing variety and contrasts. I should like to suggest that there are two qualities that the structure of a symphony will have in common with the structure of a successful radio play. The first is that of variety and contrast between different movements and between orchestral and solo passages. Secondly the great symphony will continuously delight and surprise, while at the same time seeming to fulfil an expectation on the part of the listener. It is as if in every work of art there is something that we recognise. Both symphonies and radio plays are a sound continuum, that at their best they will draw us on to a climax, a conclusion that seems inevitable. Each link in the chain will be just right in achieving this end.

A good radio play will be rich in sub-text. The number, the character and tone of voices will vary from scene to scene and there will be a varied use of sound effects. There can also be music within the scenes. The voices will usually be complemented and counterpointed by sound effects and they can be set in different acoustics; even varying for greatest contrast of acoustic between studio and location recorded scenes.

STRUCTURING A PLAY

The beginning of The World Walk
I should like to share with you, in some detail, how Jonathan Smith and I worked very closely together on his stage script of *The World Walk* to make it into a radio play.

The radio version has to attempt to accomplish at least four objectives in the first two minutes.

1. It has to give us some idea of what the play is going to be about. This is accomplished largely by the announcer, but also by the central character's, Albert Speer's, monologue.

2. It has to provide some emotional attraction, to help captivate the listener. This is done partly by the choice of music: the Horst Wessel song, a highly evocative Nazi marching tune, that is at once both uplifting and reminiscent of some of the worst atrocities of the 20th century. It is also partly done by the monologue given to Albert Speer. Although we may already know, or be beginning to surmise, that he is a convicted Nazi war criminal, we are invited to identify with him and it is difficult not to feel some sympathy for him.

3. It has to establish the conventions of the play: that we are in for a drama that is both emotional and reflective and that we shall not follow a lineal order of events, but shall jump around as memory and as apprehension dictate. It implies that we shall

be both looking back at Albert Speer's past life and forward to his forthcoming release from Spandau Prison.

4. Finally, it has to begin to stimulate some pictures in the listener's mind. Here the monologue is helped by the sound effects, in conveying our hero trudging endlessly round and round a confined space: a different kind of marching to that which we have just heard behind the Horst Wessel song.

Here are the first two minutes.

ANNOUNCER: 'The World Walk' by Jonathan Smith with John Franklyn Robbins as Albert Speer.

FADE UP AND ESTABLISH AN OLD RECORDING OF NAZI SOLDIERS MARCHING TO AND SINGING 'THE HORST WESSEL SONG', FADE DOWN:

ANNOUNCER: 'The World Walk' is based upon the book, 'Spandau, The Secret Diaries' by Albert Speer. The play is set in Spandau prison on September the 30th 1966, but the events range over a thirty-year period and do not follow chronological order. Rather, to adapt Wordsworth's idea, they are moments of time recollected in captivity and contemplated until they actually exist again. There is no ordering such thoughts; random, they come, dream-like and real. Imagine such thoughts crowding in on Speer's mind, during the last hours of his imprisonment

SWELL SONG AND THEN SLOWLY CROSSFADE WITH THE SINGLE, SOLITARY, BUT REGULAR FOOTSTEPS OF SPEER ON A GRAVEL PATH. BIRDSONG.

SPEER: (Breathing heavily from his fast pace. He has an anxious, deferential manner) Before I leave I must go and speak to Herr Hess. It won't be easy, I know that, he'll snap at me, but I must. In many ways I'd rather keep at the walk, keep myself to myself, cover a few more kilometres and prepare my mind for tomorrow. I'd rather do anything that keeps me away from that British guard Watkins and his damn fool questions. Ha – there he is near the wash house waiting for me to come round the path with that smirk on his face and as I pass he'll say, 'Still walking, Number Five?'

Answering and posing questions

That took two minutes exactly and the four aims described above have in the main been achieved. Hopefully, the listener is sufficiently enthralled to listen on. But as well as the promise of an interesting story unfolding on several levels, there is an intriguing question forming in the listener's mind: 'What is the purpose and meaning of this 'world walk' of the title?' It is a good idea in a play to both pose and to answer questions. At the same time be careful that there are not so many questions left unanswered, that the listener becomes confused and irritated and then switches off. On the other hand it is also a good idea to have some attractive questions that make the listener stay with the play in order to discover the answers. It can be a good idea, in answering one question, to pose another. Too many questions will confuse and too few will fail to intrigue the listener.

Sometimes, it can be effective to divulge information to the listener, while keeping one or two of the main characters in the dark. Then the listener has another question; 'What will happen when the character finds out? How will she or he react?'

The play continues for another minute and a half with Speer's fast and steady pace and his internal monologue. In this passage he mentions that he also has French, American and Russian guards. After 20 years of wanting to get out of prison he is suddenly afraid of his impending release. Will he be able to face everyone? Will he be able to face leaving the prison with only Hess left in it: the gravel path, the walls, the garden he has so lovingly tended? Also he will miss Anton, the medical orderly who never made him feel a criminal, who has become a friend. The thought of Anton makes him stop walking momentarily. Anton has kept him sane. Sane? Ha! He'd have gone mad without this garden path to walk round. He starts trudging again. Not that anyone would have called him sane, for walking the distance from Berlin to Mexico. And then the guard interrupts:

GUARD: (<u>Bluffly, cheerful cockney</u>) Still walking, Number Five?

SPEER: Yes, I have a little more to do.

GUARD: Round and round. The old German discipline, eh? Funny you know, I was only saying to Anton the other day, 'It won't be the same without our Mr Speer on his rounds!' And I can't think what Anton will do without you to look after.

SPEER: I can't think what I'll do without Anton.

GUARD: So all packed up and ready to go, are we?

SPEER: Yes. Not that I have much to take. Very little. Now if you'll excuse me, I must –

GUARD: (<u>Interrupting</u>) Yeah why not? Keep fit. That's the thing.

SPEER: I must go and say good-bye to Herr Hess.

GUARD: Number Seven? He's over there. Not in a very chatty mood when I last spoke to him. Having one of his off days, Number Seven is, I'd say.

SPEER: Yes, well if you'll excuse me –

GUARD: Before you go, order's just come through. The directors want to see you and Number One at nine o'clock.

SPEER: I was told ten.

GUARD: And I'm telling you nine.

SPEER: Why the change?

GUARD: It was ten o'clock, you're right. But they never agree on anything that lot. Still they wouldn't, would they? I mean, ask yourself: they put one British, one Frenchie, one Russian and one Yank in the same room and they're not likely to get much sense out of them, now are yer? Not that I said that. Still this time in honour of your release the four powers has met and they have at last agreed.

That dialogue lasted exactly one minute and five seconds. Speer marches off.

CHANGING THE STRUCTURE: SURPRISES AND DEVICES

Then, suddenly, in terms of the play's texture we have a contrast and a surprise. Such surprises, as long as they do not confuse, can heighten the listener's interest.

(AND THEN, ABRUPTLY, THE GUARD SPEAKS TO HIMSELF. HE IS A DIFFERENT MAN, QUIET, ANGRY AND BITTER. UNDERNEATH THIS INTRODUCE AN EXTENDED CHORD OF MUSIC TO ADD A QUIETLY SINISTER ATMOSPHERE)

GUARD: (INTERNAL) Go on. Walk till your knee buckles. Walk till your ticker stops and you drop. If I had my way Mr bloody, smoothy Speer you'd be here a lot longer. And inside your cell. You may have got away with your precious life at Nuremberg, but I'd like to turn the key on you myself, each night, for another twenty years. Yeah, even though it meant seeing you every day. I'd rather that than seeing you leading them all up the old garden path outside.

(WE LOSE MUSIC AND CUT TO HERR SPEER TRUDGING TOWARDS HERR HESS. BIRDSONG)

The monologue lasted 32 seconds and the play has lasted so far a total of 5 minutes, 22 seconds. It is worth noting that usually for the same number of words, monologue will play more slowly than dialogue.

SPEER: (APPROACHING) Ah, Herr Hess, would you like to join me, for a stroll?

(HERR HESS DOES NOT RESPOND. SPEER HAS ARRIVED)

SPEER: It's a nice evening, Herr Hess and I was wondering if you'd –

HESS: (Interrupts, speaking quickly and angrily) You hoping to get a job as a postman tomorrow, Herr Speer?

The scene continues. So far it is the longest in the play, lasting four and a half minutes. Hess admits that he is feeling malevolent and mischievous today. He taunts Speer about the gaggle of reporters who will be waiting for him and the fact that in the old days at the great Nazi rallies the spotlight was always on Herr Speer. Now, Herr Hess claims, all the coal delivered to Spandau will be for him alone. He doesn't of course count the scum: the guards and the orderly who look after him. He taunts Speer with being a stickler for statistics. Speer has calculated that he has walked 31,936 kilometres. Tomorrow, the day of his release, he will, in his imagination, reach Guadalajara in Mexico. He has hugely admired the Spanish colonial architecture in the Antimarac valley. It is much better, he has the humility to admit, than what he designed in the old days as Hitler's Architect in Chief. They talk particularly of the great Nazi rally of 1937 and of the trouble of erecting the big eagles that Speer designed, how pleased Hitler was with him, and how as he lowered his hand from the salute it fell smack on the bald head of Striecher. Hess roars with laughter.

HESS: The good old days, eh, Herr Speer?

SPEER: (Suddenly coldly angry) Excuse me. I must walk.

Now we are into one minute of Speer's trudging, monologue, 'The good old days! How could he?! Has he learnt nothing from the past twenty years? Calm. I must calm myself. Think of Mexico. Oh no, it's that guard again!' He is interrupted.

GUARD: Seen the papers, Herr Speer?

And we are into five and a half minutes of dialogue, in which the playwright has the guard taunt Speer by reading selected passages to him.

GUARD: 'Alone among the prisoners he has fought with all the resources of his lively mind to break through the walls of ignorance around him'.

This device conveys more information about Speer's discipline in prison and his hopes for the future and helps further to reveal the personalities of Speer and of the guard. The guard shows him a picture that must have been taken by telescopic lens. 'If they can photo you from that block of flats over there they could also shoot you, Herr Speer.'

INTRODUCING NEW CHARACTERS AND MOVING THROUGH TIME

Then Anton, the medical orderly, whose first appearance in the play we have been anticipating, arrives. Incidentally it can be both more dramatically effective and less confusing to the listeners, if they are already anticipating the introduction of a new character.

Anton tries to rescue Speer: 'Willy Brandt has sent some flowers to your daughter'.

Speer leaves Anton and the guard to argue, as defence and prosecution, about how much in his position as Reichminister for Armaments he was responsible for slave labour.

'Has he not already paid the price? Hasn't he honestly admitted his guilt?' asks Anton. 'If he's so nice how come he was involved with murderers?' taunts the guard. And we are away to Speer and into his mind again. It is marvellous how, if properly signposted, radio can instantaneously and economically change location and perspective, from the exterior world to the inside of somebody's mind.

(TRUDGING ON GRAVEL. SPEER IS BREATHING HARD. TRUDGING STOPS)

SPEER: Can't walk any more . . . that'll have to do. Damn this heart. I must lie down. At midnight I'll see them all

again – Margaret and my children, Hilde, Fritz and my
grandchildren.

For me looking back on this play, almost 20 years after I
script edited and produced it, I feel this is the first place, where
I have a criticism of the script. For the first time, almost 16
minutes into the play, the writer, it seems to me, does not manage
to convey information without sounding a little artificial or
stilted. I am sure Jonathan Smith will forgive me for this criticism.
It was his first radio play and, as script editor and producer, I
should have spotted this and made a constructive suggestion or
two.

But then he captures our interest and suspends our disbelief
again. He repeats: 'What is the truth?', a question he has asked
himself over and over again. 'Who was that young man with my
name in 1930, aged twenty five? In 1935, who was that man
leaning over the building plans with Hitler? Who was the man,
who picked up the telephone in 1942? How did I become involved
– how did you become – how did he come?' And a little later the
guard's question echoes in his mind: 'Just one thing, Number Five,
how did you become involved with murderers, with anti-Semites?'
Suddenly we are projected into the future and we are emerging
with Herr Speer from the prison, surrounded by a confusion and
cacophony of journalists' questions, culminating in the echoing:
'How does it feel to be free again?'

Thus almost 18 minutes into the play, we have what was promised at the beginning: a random moment imagined in captivity,
dream-like, yet real enough for Speer. We have momentarily
entered the future, Speer's greatest fear. Yet almost immediately,
through his memory we escape into Speer's cell, 20 years ago.
Clearly signalled and attractively orchestrated, radio can chop
about in time as much as you like.

ADDRESSING THE LISTENER

His meditation takes place within his cell. From tomorrow there
will only be one prisoner left. And then after the longest and most
effective silence so far in the script (of five seconds) for this
thought to sink in, the guard's voice intrudes again:

GUARD: (<u>Almost gentle</u>) Close your eyes if you like. Tell us some more, Herr Speer, we're all listening. We want to know.

The play subtly changes its tone. It is as if all the listeners are invited to become Speer's judges.

GUARD: We are not interested in the other prisoners, Herr Speer, we want to know about you.

As writer you need to be careful about how you choose to address the listener, if you do not wish to break the spell of the story. You can either do so at the beginning, as for example Fay Weldon does in *The Hole in the Top of the World*, or you can do so more obliquely as Jonathan Smith does here.

SPEER: If you want to understand, I must tell it my way . . . from the start . . . I liked mathematics . . . I was the best in the school . . . And rowing, as stroke . . . directing the crew . . . with my own rhythm . . . it was a marvellous feeling you know, leading and co-ordinating . . . all that power . . . There wasn't any time for cigarettes, girls . . . until I met Margaret . . . And then I remember that day I told Father I wanted to be an architect just like him, and his father. It pleased him and I liked that. We were organisers, architects. It was our tradition. A tradition I brought to shame.

There is a knock on the cell door. It is Anton come to see if all is well, to apologise for the questions of the guard. The guard leaves and Speer more easily pours out his heart to Anton. This is a very long scene in which we flash back again and again to Speer's past. It is Anton's last chance to ask many questions. It seems that he needs to understand as passionately as Speer does. 'Why is that?' we begin to wonder.

GEARING UP A PACE

The play takes on a new momentum. Speer was initially more interested in walks in the mountains and in going to the theatre than in politics. But there was poverty all around and although

Speer was not exactly poor himself, Hitler seemed to answer a struggling young architect's hopes. He met the great man and we hear the cheering and intoxicating speech-making of Hitler's rallies, backed by triumphal Wagnerian music. Hitler employs him as his chief architect. Speer works day and night and hardly sees his family. He is reproached by his father, a gentle, disappointed voice from another era, for being part of a new madness; and by his wife for only being known by the children as 'the man who brings sweets'. We begin to see how the 'good, family man' can become corrupted.

And then we leap forward and we learn of Speer's growing disillusion and of his confession to Hess, while walking round the prison garden, of how he planned to kill Hitler.

The elements of the play are all working in unison, now, to drive the story forward and unpeel Speer's character layer by layer, so that we, the listeners can share with Speer a better understanding.

After his attempt to kill Hitler failed in late 1944, Speer's vision becomes apocalyptic, like something out of Hieronymus Bosch.

SPEER: His skin gradually fell away from his face when he spoke to me and I saw a dark stain right down his body . . . And I couldn't see why I had joined the dance. Oh God!

And we flash forward to a few years ago in his cell when it is Anton knocking on the door as he did a few moments previously. It is remarkable how powerful a simple sound effect such as this can be on radio. Anton sees that he is depressed and becomes his saviour, by smuggling extra toilet paper into him.

ANTON: Your leg needs a lot of bandage for a good few months in my medical opinion.

His writing will be hidden there to escape the shredder of the Russian guard. He can begin to seek out the truth, eventually to communicate again with the outside world. To a captive this can feel like freedom. (Author's note: I have recently experienced this in helping prisoners to write and produce radio plays.)

From now on the play becomes more and more free ranging. Speer in prison is on trial, not just from the guard, from Anton and from his own conscience, but also from his fellow prisoners for admitting too much guilt at his trial by the Allies and thus betraying the ideals of the Nazism, which many of them still maintain.

The author has set up a convention in which he can roam wherever he likes in Speer's life, driven by the overwhelming compulsion to get at the truth – whatever that is. It makes powerful listening.

Anton becomes much more insistent in his questioning than would seem appropriate for a simple medical orderly. Speer does not appear to be suspicious. He is glad to have an interrogator who is sympathetic and as meticulous for detail as himself. However, we the listeners must begin to become suspicious. This is yet another dramatic device, to keep us listening.

USING MUSIC

About 50 minutes into this 90-minute play Anton takes his leave, closing the door with a resounding echo and leaving Speer, for the last time, before his release tomorrow, to his solitary soul searching:

SPEER: . . . But I am a criminal.

(INTRODUCE ETHEREAL AND SOOTHING MUSIC UNDER SPEER'S MONOLOGUE)

SPEER: For years I went to the Chapel services. The Chaplain played Bruckner on the gramophone and I moved closer to my family.

(THE MOCKING VOICES OF THE FELLOW PRISONERS, ADMIRAL DOENITZ AND HITLER YOUTH LEADER, SCHIRACH INTRUDE)

DOENITZ AND   I should pray, Herr Speer, as much as you
SCHIRACH: can.

(THE MUSIC DROWNS THEM OUT AND THEN STOPS)

SPEER: And I tried to pray.

The effect of music cannot be overestimated in radio drama. Here it creates a wonderfully soothing effect. Also Speer himself uses it to blot out his tormentors; but as if he had tried too hard he destroys the music and he is left again, arid, vainly seeking solace, trying to pray.

One can use music in several ways, but should beware the danger of suddenly seeming to introduce a full orchestra into the same setting as the characters. One can establish the convention at the beginning, that music from a particular symphony is intrinsic to a central character's emotional make-up. This way the listener will recognise and accept the shorthand whenever it is introduced. Alternatively one can, as Speer does here, mention the occasion on which the music is played, and use it to echo in the mind thereafter.

RACING AGAINST THE CLOCK

The play continues with an agonising meeting in prison with his wife Margaret. He is only allowed one minute and ten seconds and a British officer has to be present. She tells him that his mother is paralysed from a stroke, but how she had loved the drawings he had sent her, how she had said he might become a second Dürer.

SPEER: When I last saw her, Father shook my hand, but she held back as if I were unclean.

They speak briefly of the children. Margaret tells him that Ernst is having a difficult time at school. And time is up, the interview is over.

It is amazing how skilfully Jonathan Smith manages to invite our insight into and sympathy for this 'good family-man', who became a war criminal, responsible for employing millions in slave labour camps.

INTRODUCING COMEDY

In such a relentlessly compelling play, it is important to have moments of comedy. And Jonathan Smith provides them. There is the comic outrage of his fellow prisoners when the Prison Chaplain compares them to lepers; and a marvellous scene when the French guard suggests sharing the hundred thousand marks reward for finding the disappeared Nazi criminal, Martin Boorman. Speer decides suddenly to pretend that really the French guard is Boorman in disguise: the face, the stocky figure, the hair that has been dyed and the French accent that never really rang true. With wild humour and close to breaking point, he screams around the prison that really Sadot, the French guard, is none other than Martin Boorman!

After the Martin Boorman and the leper incidents, he is silent for weeks, trudging round and round the gardens, keeping sane by meticulously charting his imagined 'World Walk'. He is approaching the Bering Strait between Siberia and Alaska. Often he is accompanied by Hess, who occasionally breaks the silence:

HESS: One of these days they'll make a good technicolour movie about us. (He giggles) Make sure the actor who plays you, Herr Speer, wears a halo.

SPEER: Oh my God! I must have been wandering. I've miscalculated. It's July! The current will have melted everything. We're already out to sea! What am I going to do?

HESS: I'm all right on this ice floe.

This set-back to his plans makes him compensate by getting down to frantic writing about the slave-labour plan. He becomes obsessive. He has a weak heart which we begin to hear beating as more and more questions about the final solution crowd in on him. He falls into a sleep, climaxing in a nightmare in which, amidst a cacophony of guards' footsteps, slamming cell doors and a litany of the names of the condemned, he thinks the executioners are coming for him.

REACHING THE CLIMAX OF THE PLAY

We are nearing the climax of the play. Anton on the last night admits that he was one of Speer's slave-labourers. He assumes the role of Speer's judge. 'Let me remind you', he says 'of those films shown at Nuremberg.' We hear the noise of the film running through its spools. The film's calm, measured commentary on the statistics of the dead, interweaves with Anton's interrogation.

Speer's final statement:

SPEER: I am grateful and ashamed of my life. I am ashamed and grateful for my imprisonment. And now if you will excuse me I must walk a little.

The guard's final statement, in reply to the releasing officer:

GUARD: If he was the best of the bunch, he must have been the worst.

The play ends with Speer being released from the prison gates to be met by the full force of the paparazzi. Whether or not this is true freedom and whether or not Albert Speer has expiated his guilt is left for us, the listeners, to decide.

We have spent a long time on this single, 90-minute play, but this analysis should help to cast light on many of the points made in the rest of the book. The analysis was intentionally more thorough at the beginning, where the playwright was putting together the elements and establishing the conventions that he would use again and again throughout the play. Hopefully one day it will be possible to record a new production of this play, that you, the listener, might download from the Internet.

4

Exploring Language and Belief

USING WORDS AS FLYING SCULPTURES

This chapter is not about the connection between conventional religious belief and language, but about how language properly employed can make the listener participate and believe in a reality beyond the mundane and the everyday. The power of speech can invest the ordinary and familiar experiences of life with humour, meaning, grief, joy and enchantment, that we might not otherwise glimpse.

The most ancient form of story telling, aeons before the invention of writing, was the oral tradition. The earliest story tellers, through their skill and their magic, would conjure up pictures that cave dwellers would see in the flames of the fire that warmed them at night and kept away wild animals. Druid story tellers would memorise by heart thousands of lines of narrative verse. As late as Shakespeare's day most story telling was by word of mouth and his audience was far more sensitive to the nuances and resonances of the human voice than we are in this, our literary and our visual age.

D G Bridson, a radio drama producer in the 1940s and 1950s, pointed out in his memoir, *Prospero and Ariel*, that 'Not many of us can teach ourselves to write until we teach ourselves to talk'. His contemporary, Donald McWhinnie, suggested how we should prepare to listen to radio: 'Sit in a dark room and talk and listen. Even if you are not vitally interested in words, they suddenly acquire a compulsion of meaning they did not have before; they develop a richness of texture through being isolated, and you focus your sensibility and imagination on them as you rarely do in daylight.'

The French poet, Paul Claudel, employed a vivid image to describe this tangible power. For him a word was made by mouthed gestures. He talked of the breath of life, 'inspired' or breathed into us by God. This we in turn 'expire' in the form of vowels shaped with our lips, tongue and teeth to form consonants and so model words, which we expel into the air in the form of 'flying sculptures'. This is a wonderful French conceit, but one that echoes in my mind when I hear poetry really well delivered. Many years ago I had the privilege of producing Paul Scofield reading Gerard Manley Hopkins' *The Wreck Of The Deutschland*:

> Thou mastering me
> God! giver of breath and bread;
> World's strand, sway of the sea;
> Lord of living and dead;
> Thou hast bound bones and veins in me, fastened me flesh,
> And after it almost unmade, what with dread
> Thy doing: and dost thou touch me afresh?
> Over again I feel thy finger and find thee.

This and the 25 subsequent stanzas were a magnificent procession of flying sculptures!

UNDERSTANDING WHAT THE WORD HAS TO ACCOMPLISH

In radio, as a writer you will need to be at the same time both more economical and more imaginative than you would be on the page. A reader can skim through paragraphs of description. He can put down and pick up the book; ruminate and recap. None of this can happen in the continuum of a radio play. Even on cassette it is inconvenient. Thus you will need to learn to describe scenery and people and to express depth of feeling, implicitly and obliquely and in a matter of seconds.

Giles Cooper does so in the following excerpt from *Without the Grail*. In a few sentences he establishes an atmosphere of heat and exhaustion, vividly paints the locale where most of the action is to take place, carries his plot a stage forward, gives a new insight into his leading character – and at the same time diverts us with humour and suspense. The writing is pared to the bone. When performed it is rich in overtones.

(FADE IN CAR RUNNING: IT SLOWS AND STOPS.)

(PAUSE.)

INNES: What's the matter?

INDIAN DRIVER: Stop to cool the engine.

INNES: Okay, you're the driver. (PAUSE.) So this is the jungle.

DRIVER: Yes, all jungle here.

INNES: H'm – Very dusty looking.

DRIVER: The road is making it dusty. Inside is green.

(PAUSE.)

INNES: There's a railway line over there. Where does it go?

DRIVER: No place. Into the jungle, stop.

INNES: Eh? – Why?

DRIVER: Military reasons. Now abandoned.

INNES: Wartime?

DRIVER: Yes, wartime. In Assam there were armies all the time. Now in the jungle here live all things.

INNES: Er – animals, you mean?

DRIVER: No, *things*. Wheels and chains gone rusting. Old guns and tanks not moving. In one place were fifty thousand teeth-brush, abandoned. All abandoned.

(PAUSE.)

(CAR STARTS AND MOVES OFF. FADE OUT.)

The car tells us that we are moving in and out of the scene. The rest is done by language.

RELEASING THE POETRY FROM YOUR PROSE

At the risk of sounding academic, I should like to examine why in *Julius Caesar* after the assassination of Caesar, Shakespeare has Brutus address the Roman crowd in prose and Anthony address them in poetry. I first approached this question practically, through directing drama students. I surmised that Shakespeare made this distinction, because prose is more tentative and lacks the authority, the confidence and the natural beauty of poetry. He knew that poetry would be more persuasive and powerful and would help Anthony to captivate and convince the Roman populace, at the expense of Brutus and of Cassius.

In a sense much excellent spoken prose contains elements of poetry and in my time working with writers, I have come to the romantic conclusion that each of us has an 'original and unique voice', a sense of poetry waiting to be unlocked. Once or twice I have been rewarded by hearing writers develop from the mundane, prosaic and stilted and take wing with original, beautiful and arresting language. They have found their voice.

You as a writer, having accomplished this, have to help the actor to lift it off the page and in this respect I should like to give you a tip that I learnt from Peter Tinniswood. I noticed in the first script of his that I worked on that he had set it out in a particular way. He was gratified when I spotted this. I promised that the BBC typist would reflect the same layout in the production script.

Here is an example of what I mean from the beginning of his award winning play, *The Village Fete*:

NANCY:	We moved from London to the country on a
[TO MIKE].	misty morning in early May.
	There were no blackheaded gulls.
	Thrushes sang.
	Next door neighbour's cat howled.
	And the house spider came out from his hole by the fireplace in the drawing-room to bid us all good-bye.
	He seemed so smug about it all.
	The removal men couldn't park outside the house.
	But, of course.
	William got distraught.
	But, of course.

WILLIAM: [ALOUD]	It's so outrageously inconvenient.
ROSIE:	Moving house is always inconvenient, William.
WILLIAM:	But it's specifically inconvenient to me, Rosie. I'm approaching the climax of my book. It's all locked away in my head. I am rapidly approaching the dénouement. Do you understand? The dénouement. And this move will destroy it.

The actor has to work very fast. He has to lift the words off the page, deliver them, monitor how he is saying them and attempt to make them even more spontaneous, truthful and interesting. The actors have to listen to each other and use each other's energy. They have to respond to each other's pitch, timing and tone. The layout on the page is crucial. Peter Tinniswood's trick of the trade certainly helps.

WORKING WITHOUT VISUAL AIDS

See how many pictures there were in the passage from *The Village Fete*. Compare it with this passage from Timothy West's wonderful spoof on how *not* to write a radio play: *This Gun That I Have In My Right Hand Is Loaded*.

LAURA: What's that you've got under your arm, Clive?

CLIVE: It's an evening paper, Laura.

(PAPER NOISE)

I've just been reading about the Oppenheimer smuggling case. Good gracious, it's nice to sit down after that long train journey from the insurance office in the city.

LAURA: Let me get you a drink, Clive darling.

(LENGTHY POURING, CLINK)

CLIVE: Thank you, Laura my dear.

(CLINK, SIP, GULP)

Aah, Amontillado eh? Good stuff. What are you having?

LAURA: I'll think I'll have a whisky, if it's all the same to you.

(CLINK, POURING, SYPHON)

CLIVE: Whisky, eh? That's a strange drink for an attractive, auburn-haired girl of twenty nine – anything wrong?

LAURA: No, it's nothing, Clive, I –

CLIVE: Yes?

LAURA: No, really, I –

CLIVE: You're my wife, Laura. Whatever it is you can tell me. I'm your husband.

This may be a grossly unfair comparison, but it can illustrate some useful points. Peter Tinniswood's passage of almost exactly as many words has many more interesting, original and beautiful images. I count at least nine in Nancy's first speech. How, exactly, a house spider can look smug, I am not sure, but my imagination is working on it. Not only are there far fewer images in *This Gun* . . . , but they are spelt out in an (intentionally) stilted and clumsy way.

Colin Haydn Evans in his book, *Writing For Radio*, said that if you want to understand how radio drama works listen to as many bad radio plays as possible. In good plays it is sometimes difficult to see the sleight of hand by which it is done, to see where the seams are. If you listen to bad plays, you can see that the technique shows all too transparently and you can see what not to do. No doubt when he came to write this script, Timothy West had worked on too many radio plays that creaked, in which the writers had not mastered the art of obliquely drawing pictures.

Anyway, I recommend that you listen to as many radio plays as possible. You will hear both good and bad.

SUSPENDING DISBELIEF

I should now like to give you an illustration from *Of The Levitation At St Michael's* by Carey Harrison, a play that both portrays something you have probably never seen and should also help you to suspend disbelief in such a phenomenon. It is a two-hander about a couple of goatkeepers in East Anglia. One of them, Elizabeth, acts as the narrator:

ELIZABETH: We were going on an errand of mercy, to examine a sick goat owned by a novice goat-keeper. A passion for goats was about the only thing I shared in common with Matty; that, and the sheer pleasure of getting away, from time to time. For an hour or two. Matty had a husband, Ted; a backward child – to be precise, a Mongol child – called Winston; and the finest herd of goats in East Anglia.

MATTY CAN BE HEARD, STOMPING THROUGH THE MUD TOWARDS ELIZABETH'S CAR, MUTTERING DARKLY

ELIZABETH: I had a husband: Jack. No children. One or two reasonably good goats. Prize-winners.

After a dialogue scene as they set off in the car, she continues:

ELIZABETH: We were an unlikely pair, to tell the truth. But livestock brings people together across all sorts of social barriers. And – temperamental ones too. Matty and I were very different kinds of goatkeeper. She was a goat breeder; a pro. I was an amateur. Encouraged by my husband. Though not out of love. Years ago when Jack first stood for Parliament, the local television people came and filmed me milking a goat – at Jack's request. The common touch, to impress the locals.

Later Matty and Elizabeth, having lost the address of where they are supposed to be going, end up visiting a remote Ghilbertine Abbey chapel instead. It is this passage that invites the listener to suspend disbelief in a seemingly supernatural phenomenon.

MATTY:　　　　Well it's a lovely place. It makes you *want* to pray. And never mind the colours.

(MATTY MEANS NOTHING OF THE KIND; SHE CERTAINLY DOESN'T FIND IT 'LOVELY'; AS ELIZABETH IS WELL AWARE. A MOMENT'S PAUSE)

Incidentally this direction, about how the words should be delivered, is skilfully placed in the script. If such a chunk came within the speech, it might deflect the actor, momentarily but crucially, from making the line her own and from getting the timing right. A single word's direction as in the next speech is not such a problem, though even here it is a good idea not to bombard the actor with too many notes (both on and off the page!). My advice would only be to give 'how to interpret' instructions when it is not obvious to the intelligent and intuitive actor.

Elizabeth in turn suggests that Matty might say a prayer, but soon regrets her suggestion.

MATTY:　　　　Pray for Winston? That wouldn't do much good, would it? He's going to die soon – you know that. They all do. They don't often reach thirty.

ELIZABETH:　　Yes – I didn't really mean that, Matty –

MATTY:　　　　What then? Just – put in a word for him, seeing he'll be coming up for judgement shortly. Is that it? Almighty God: remember Winston.

(ELIZABETH SAYS NOTHING)

MATTY:　　　　What? Remember Winston?

ELIZABETH: I'm sure he does.

MATTY: What? I should think He *does*! If anyone bloody
                sent him into the world, He did. He knows! If
                He was going to *do* something about it – He
                won't need to be reminded, will He!

(AS MATTY'S VOICE RISES, THE ECHOES BOOM
AROUND THE WALLS)

ELIZABETH: (COWED) No, of course not.

MATTY: *What* then? What am I supposed to do, then?
                Ask for something? Pray for something? Any-
                thing I want at all? Send me a helper, Lord.
                Another idiot. Just for a lark send me a bloody
                half-wit for a husband. Oh *He knows*!

(A MOMENT'S PAUSE)

MATTY: Shall I give him the pleasure, then? Come on,
                you tell me! What do I say? Thank you, Lord
                for giving me a monster, for choosing me, thank
                you, wonderful LORD. Is that it? Thank you,
                sweet Jesus, it's your chosen mother speaking –

(AS MATTY RANTS, MUSIC RETURNS, ONE HELD
NOTE, SWELLING)

ELIZABETH: (CLOSE; TO US) She was lit up with rage,
                appalling.

MATTY: Do you think he wants me crawling back for
                help? Do you? Now? When I've had twenty
                years of it? Do you? Please God! He'd bloody
                laugh at me! (Self-mocking) O Lord – thank you
                for picking me, what did I do, did I offend You?
                (Thunderously) Offend me? Ha ha ha you silly
                woman!

ELIZABETH: (CLOSE, AS THE NOTE SWELLS) Then it
                happened. Then it began: quite gradually. Oh, it

was comic at first, her fat little body there in the middle of an aisle; lifting up into the air. Matty floating in mid-air. But the laughter stuck in my throat. By the time she was fully two foot off the ground, all I could do was gape. Her voice had trailed away. How long had we been silent? I was staring. She was looking down; mouth open, silent. Fat little legs; not swinging; stiff. I saw it clearly. I felt dizzy. Then she spoke.

(MATTY'S VOICE COMES, HOARSE, FRIGHTENED)

MATTY: Help – me –

(THE NOTE STILL HELD, HIGH IN THE AIR)

ELIZABETH: I rose to help her. Did I rise?

(A HEAVY SOUND: SOMEONE FALLING. THE NOTE BREAKS OFF. FOOTSTEPS; RUNNING. MATTY'S VOICE, HARSH, COMING CLOSER, AS SHE RUNS OVER TO ELIZABETH)

MATTY: Elizabeth! Elizabeth!

(SILENCE. THE ECHOES FADE. THE OUTDOOR ACOUSTIC RETURNS. BREATHING; PANTING)

ELIZABETH: Stop.

MATTY: What's the matter?

ELIZABETH: It's my hat. I've left my hat inside. My woolly hat. It must have fallen off.

MATTY: Come on, then. We'll go back.

ELIZABETH: All right.

(HER TONE MAKES MATTY PAUSE)

MATTY: You still look a bit queer. You stay. I'll go back and fetch it.

ELIZABETH: No. Leave it.

MATTY: What? That's a nice hat.

ELIZABETH: Leave it.

MATTY: You just want to leave it there? (<u>A moment's pause. She tuts mildly</u>) Some people – that's a nice hat.

ELIZABETH: Did I black out, or what? I must have fainted.

MATTY: You fainted all right. Passed clean out.

ELIZABETH: Matty . . . what happened?

MATTY: I sat you up. You came round fast enough.

ELIZABETH: Before I fainted. What happened?

MATTY: (<u>Blandly</u>) *I* don't know, dear. It was most peculiar, *I* can tell you.

ELIZABETH: You were. (<u>She chokes on a nervous laugh</u>) you were – sort of floating.

MATTY: (<u>As before</u>) Was I? I can remember looking down. It scared me for a moment. Everything looked different. Stretched.

ELIZABETH: Stretched?

MATTY: I was floating was I? How d'you mean?

ELIZABETH: Above the ground.

MATTY: Floating above the ground. No wonder everything looked funny.

(ABRUPTLY MATTY BREAKS INTO A RAUCOUS CHUCKLE)

MATTY: It's a bloody miracle, then.

I have quoted from this play at some length, because I should like you to think about the structure. The author has not introduced us to the world of the supernatural at the beginning. On the contrary, we have inhabited a naturalistic world of amused scepticism. However, because of the contrasting attitudes of the two characters – of disbelief at what she has seen on Elizabeth's part and of dismissal on Matty's – I think the author plays a clever confidence trick on the listener. The listener is drawn into the situation and probably accepts that Matty *really* has been suspended in the air.

5

Using Scenes, Music, Sound Effects and Silence

DEFINING A RADIO SCENE

There are two ways of defining scenes in radio: from the listener's and from the producer's point of view. For the listener a new scene happens when there is a change of location or a shift in time. It may for example be a shift from first person narration to a dialogue during a storm at sea, or a flashback from a mother and daughter talking today to the mother and *her* mother talking 25 years ago.

From the director's point of view a scene will be a chunk of the play that is convenient to record in one go and, as a director, I will often mark up the author's script in this way, to make clear my intentions to the technicians. However, I will be as careful as I can never to meddle with the author's intentions.

BEGINNING AND ENDING A RADIO SCENE

The opening scenes of Fay Weldon's play, *Polaris*, alternate between the interior of a submarine and the home of Meg, the pregnant wife of one of the naval officers. I shall give you a couple of ins and outs from one scene to another, showing how the next scene is set up, using language, music and sound effects in an entertaining and economic way. This is how the play starts:

(WE ARE IN THE CONTROL ROOM OF A POLARIS SUBMARINE, IN DOCK, ON THE SURFACE. THE CAPTAIN AND JIM, THE FIRST LIEUTENANT, ARE COMPLETING A DAILY-USER CHECK, AND EXCHANGING A MURMURED CONVERSATION OVER ASSORTED WHIRRS, CLICKS AND THE SOUND OF RADIO 1: 'RUDOLPH THE RED-NOSED REINDEER'. THE CAPTAIN IS A SUAVE AND EASY FELLOW: RATHER TOO MUCH SO FOR HIS FIRST

LIEUTENANT.

CAPTAIN: Hydroplane system. One-man-control?

JIM: A OK, sir –

CAPTAIN: Plotting tables?

JIM: All complete, sir –

CAPTAIN: Sounder?

JIM: Hold on, sir –

(SILENCE. THEN PING-PING-PING FROM THE ECHO SOUNDER)

JIM: A OK, sir –

(THAT SEEMS TO BE THAT. THE PLAY PROPER, AS IT WERE, BEGINS)

Let us skip forward to the ending of the first and the beginning of the second scene:

JIM: Cold out there, sir. Snug as a bug in here.

CAPTAIN: Snug as a bug. User check complete. Down periscope. Goodbye, God's eye. See you in three months. Take care. Small you said (*referring to Tim, the Navigator's wife*), and learning to be sensible. Ah!

(RADIO 4: 'DECK THE HALLS WITH BOUGHS OF HOLLY')

CAPTAIN: She won't be lonely?

JIM: They have a dog.

(CUT TO: THOMPSON, THE DOG, HALF SPRINGER, HALF ALSATIAN, WHICH MAKES HIM AMIABLE

AND ENORMOUS, SLURPS AND GRUNTS OVER THE
SLEEPING MEG'S FACE. THE BEDSIDE RADIO IS
TUNED TO RADIO 4 AND CONTINUES FROM THE
PREVIOUS SCENE IN THE NEW ACOUSTIC. RADIO
4: ' 'TIS THE SEASON TO BE JOLLY')

THOMPSON: Phloph

MEG: Go away, Thompson. Get off this bed. You're
              not allowed on the bed. Get off! Timmy, get
              him off. Timmy? Oh, Timmy, you're gone. I
              forgot. Three months. Oh Thompson, you
              stupid dog, what will I do? Sleep. ' 'Tis the
              season to be jolly.'

Thus Fay Weldon invents some call signs to signal where we are
going: the ping-ping of the echo sounder, the Christmas songs on
Radios 1 and 4 and the slobbering of Thompson. This is the next
scene change:

POSTMAN: You're too isolated up here. You'd have done
              better to have chosen nearer to the Base with
              the others. But that's your affair.

    (HE GOES)

MEG: I didn't want to be near the others. I wanted us
              all alone, just the two of us. Oh, Timmy.
              'God rest you merry, gentlemen,
              Let nothing you dismay.'

    (THOMPSON JOINS IN, HOWLING)

              Be quiet, Thompson, you stupid dumb dog. If
              you could talk there'd be some point to you.

    (SLIGHT EDGE OUT. DOWN IN THE POLARIS: PING-
    PING-PING)

CAPTAIN: 'God rest you merry, gentlemen,
              Let nothing you dismay' –

> Glad to see you, Timmy. Now perhaps we can get on with the fast cruise.

TIMMY: Morning, sir. I was last aboard. That's never happened before.

CAPTAIN: You've never been married before.
'Remember Christ our Saviour
Was born on Christmas day' –

Normally a playwright will wish to hide his hand as an artist. However, in the next example, the writer plays with the ambiguity of similarly sounding words. Within a half-hour comedy of five scenes, the playwright starts three of them with different meanings of the same sound.

<u>INDONESIAN GAMELAN MUSIC ON LOVE'S AND FLO'S HI-FI SYSTEM</u>

ANNOUNCER: We present 'A To B and Back Again' by Nick Pullin, with Christian Rodska as Love and Liz Goulding as Flo.

<u>MIX MUSIC INTO SCENE 1: LOVE'S LOUD SIPPING AND SLURPING HIS DRINK.</u>

LOVE: Wales!

FLO: North – or like south?

LOVE: North. I mean there's fewer people. Less cars.

FLO: That's right.

LOVE: I mean, can't you just see all that clean air? You know.

FLO: I know.

LOVE: I mean, we could get a goat. (*and so on*)

SCENE 3 ALSO STARTS WITH GAMELAN MUSIC AND LOVE SLURPING

FLO: Whales?

LOVE: Oh, yeah

FLO: What like . . .

LOVE: Migrating. They swim past the coast every year. Hump backs, blues, sperm.

FLO: Oh – is it clean? (*and so on*)

SCENE 4. DIDGERIDOO MUSIC ON HI-FI SYSTEM AND LOVE SLURPING

KEV: Wails!

LOVE: What?

KEV: Wails! He's on my lap, right. And he just sits there and wails. Cries his bloody eyes out.

The repetition of words of the same or similar sound is not unlike the use of music to link scenes.

USING MUSIC IN RADIO DRAMA

Perhaps the most obvious use of music in radio drama is in a play about a composer's life. Playwright Bruce Stewart began *Symphonic Variations* about the elderly César Franck's love for the young Irish composer, Augusta Holmes, with one of the most romantic pieces of music ever written. Being a married man and a strict Catholic, Franck poured his passion into a composition that was not at all his usual style. In that way he sublimated what might otherwise have become an adulterous affair.

(THE BEGINNING OF THE FIRST MOVEMENT OF CESAR FRANCK'S PIANO QUINTET. AFTER 15

SECONDS FADE AND KEEP UNDER HIS
MONOLOGUE)

CESAR: Oh my soul! My love! Only in music shall I reach out
to you. Only in music shall we become as one. We shall
identify, conjoin, like light from the far stars, shining,
enduring, as long as music itself. My soul, my love, my
Augusta!

(SWELL MUSIC)

Music can be used in many ways. It can swing you instantaneously
from one mood to another. It can – as subtly as a raised eyebrow –
give to a phrase an extra, and possibly contradictory, level
of meaning. It can provide unity, where unity may otherwise
be difficult to achieve. Simple counterpoint, perhaps using one
instrument, like the zither in Carol Reed's *The Third Man*, can be
very effective.

I should like to give you an example that with the appropriate
texts and compact discs you can try out for yourself. Such preparation is your responsibility as a radio playwright.

I have twice produced *A Midsummer Night's Dream* with the
students of the Bristol Old Vic Theatre School for local radio. I
had in mind Chesterton's description that the play is about 'the
mysticism of happiness'. On each occasion, I chose some French
romantic music that seemed admirably to convey this sentiment.

I am strict with the students over the delivery of the verse. If
the actor gets the metre and the timing right, then the pictures,
the emotions and the meaning come alive. I fed the music to the
actors through earphones, so that it would not be picked up by the
microphone. This meant I could fine tune and adjust the levels in
post production. I said to them, 'This is giving you the emotional
content. However, I want you to counterpoint the rhythm, so
that you really strive to be faithful to Shakespeare's verse.' The
experiment proved more successful than I had imagined.

At the time of my first production I still had César Franck's
Piano Quintet echoing in my mind. I first introduced it to help
exaggerate Helena's unrequited longing for Demetrius. Having
established this convention, I used the same piece of music as the
lovers' theme at several crucial points. The greater the pangs of
love, the greater the comedy:

(ESTABLISH THE PIANO QUINTET AND THEN
FADE BUT KEEP UNDER THE SPEECH)

HELENA: How happy some o'er other some can be!
          Through Athens I am thought as fair as she.
          But what of that? Demetrius thinks not so . . .
          (*and so on*)

We kept it, softly, under the whole speech and swelled it at the
end.

I wanted to do something similar with the fairies and was
fortunate to find a marvellous CD collection of music for oboe
and guitar. This gave me a unity for the fairies and for the royal
couple, who are to be wedded. I chose Jacque Ibert's *Entr'acte* for
Peaseblossom and for Puck. Ibert is a delicate and witty composer
and this piece has the right quicksilver quality:

PEASEBLOSSOM: Over hill, over dale,
                  Thorough bush, thorough brier,
                Over park, over pale,
                  Thorough flood, thorough fire,
                I do wander every where,
                  Swifter than the moon's sphere . . . (*and
                so on*)

Then for Titania's and Oberon's famous confrontation:

OBERON: Ill met by moonlight, proud Titania.

TITANIA: What, jealous Oberon! Fairies, skip hence;
           I have forsworn his bed and company.

OBERON: Tarry, rash wanton; am not I thy lord . . . ? (*and
           so on*)

I chose Erik Satie's *Gnossienne No 1*. To my ear it has the
stateliness of a royal dance, while at the same time possessing
something both whimsical and threatening. I also found a regal
and mysterious piece called *La Romanesca* by Fernando Sor. This
I used as the title music, to go behind the credits and to introduce
the court of Theseus. Finally for the mechanicals, Bottom, Quince

and the gang, I had some gifted and inventive students form a skiffle band and improvise their own comic music.

Music can be a wonderful shorthand in introducing and reminding us of an emotion, a character or a picture. The more thought the writer gives to it, the more the director has to build upon. Sometimes one may be able to afford a composer and some instrumentalists. Most broadcasting companies have an agreement with the Performing Rights Society, whereby they are authorised to use excerpts from commercial recordings of music. If, however, you are selling your script to a cassette distributor, you will need to be very careful about the copyright laws.

USING SOUND EFFECTS

The theatre director, Tyrone Guthrie, wrote several radio plays. He said the writer should be responsible for the entire sound pattern. In his play *The Flowers Are Not For You To Pick* he described the sound of a non-naturalistic sea: 'By its rhythms and tone it may be possible to suggest not merely the water in which our hero is engulfed, but the beating of the heart, the tumult of fear, the immutable laws and irresistible strength of nature compared with our puny and inconstant selves.' I can imagine the creative Elizabeth Parker, late of the BBC's Radiophonic Workshop, rising to such a challenge.

Most sound effects are far more straightforward than the above. I suggest to writers that they should be minimal. As Matisse, in his drawings, leaves the viewer to fill in the outlines, so one should give the listener just enough to trigger the imagination. The greatest number of complaints that one receives from listeners is about plays that are swamped by sound effects or about a level of music that drowns out the nuances of language. I remember Peter Tinniswood, in an actor's narration, writing: 'Winston knocked on the door'. An over enthusiastic and literal-minded studio manager provided the sound effect of knocking on a studio door. Peter and I asked, 'What are you doing? It's already there in the listener's head. Let's only have the sound effect of the door opening, before the dialogue commences.'

Incidentally I hate doors in radio plays. I usually ask writers to lose all openings and closings that are not vital for information or for dramatic effect. On the other hand, I like to have fun with sound effects. In Carey Harrison's *I Never Killed my German* there is a moment when we hear the sound of what could be tapping on a hollow wooden box. Willy Benefer, first person narrator says: ' "It's all in there," I said, tapping my brainbox . . .'

USING SILENCE

How long you hold a pause, how you fade in and out of scenes, how long you give the listener to form an image in his mind or digest a thought or feeling can be very important. There is not much more to be said about this, except that comparative silence, that is, how you travel from full volume to absolute silence and back again, is an important part of a writer's armoury.

6

Creating Character and Comedy

DECIDING HOW MANY CHARACTERS TO HAVE IN YOUR PLAY

How many characters can appear in a play is a question often asked by newcomers to radio drama. There are four points to bear in mind:

1. The listener will only 'see' characters if they are described or if they are identified by speaking or being spoken to. It is no good putting in the directions that a character is present in a scene or sequence and expecting the listener to read the writer's mind, to know this by magic.

2. It is easy to confuse the listener by having too many characters in a scene. If you read the following (abridged) excerpt from *This Gun That I Have In My Left Hand Is Loaded* and try to see and commit to memory all the characters introduced, I think you will take my point.

(FADE IN PUB NOISES)

HAWKINS:	(Middle-aged, cheerful Londoner) Evening, Mabel. Busy tonight, isn't it.
BARMAID:	It certainly is, Mr Hawkins. I've been on my feet all evening.
FARRELL:	(Approaching, middle-aged, cheerful Londoner) Evening, George, what are you having?
HAWKINS:	A pint of the usual, please.
FARRELL:	Two pints of the usual, please, Mabel.
BARMAID:	(OFF) Coming up, Mr Farrell.

HAWKINS: Evening, Norman.

JACKSON: (<u>Middle-aged, cheerful, Londoner</u>) Hello there, George. What are you having, Bert?

FARRELL: I'm just getting them, Norman.

JACKSON: Well, leave me out, I'm getting one for Charlie Illingworth. Two halves of the usual, Mabel.

BAINES: (<u>Coming up, middle-aged, cheerful, Londoner</u>) Evening, all.

JACKSON: Hello, Arnold, haven't seen you in ages.

BARMAID: Your change, Mr Farrell.

FARRELL: Thanks, Mabel. Where's Charlie got to? Ah, there you are, Charlie. You know Arnold Baines, don't you?

ILLING: (<u>Cheerful, Londoner, middle-aged</u>) Known the old so-and-so for ages. What'll you have?

JACKSON: No, no, I'm getting them. What is it?

BAINES: Oh, I'll just have my usual, thanks.

JACKSON: Who's looking after you, George, old man?

BARMAID: There's yours, Mr Hawkins.

MR HAWKINS: Bung ho!

FARRELL: Cheers, George.

BAINES: Cheers, Norman.

JACKSON: Cheers, Bert.

ILLING: Cheers, Arnold.

3. Just as in language you need to be as economical as you can, to allow each speech to accomplish as many functions as possible, so I recommend most writers to have as few characters as they absolutely need. This will save on the production budget, but, more importantly, listeners will tend to be more interested in, and to identify with characters who develop throughout a play and who appear in more than one scene.

   I sometimes suggest to aspiring writers that they should combine two relatively minor characters into one more rounded and interesting character.

4. Again the fewer characters you have within a play, the more there will be for each actor to get his teeth into. Although this may mean that there are fewer parts overall, at least those actors that are in work should have a more fulfilling time.

While on the subject of actors, I think it can be a very useful exercise for a playwright to write a short biography and background of each of his characters. This can be helpful in providing insight and interpretation for the director and actors, who have to work very fast in radio. It may also help you, the playwright, to gain insight into, and to provide richness and sub-text for, your characters.

WHY CHARACTER AND COMEDY?

I believe that in radio drama the revealing of character and what it is that moves the listener to laughter have much in common. I first came to the conclusion that the best radio comedy takes the form of a gradual recognition on the part of the listener, many years ago, when I produced a series of autobiographical comedies by the probation officer and journalist, Geoffrey Parkinson. They are the most appealing and compassionate kind of comedy, in which the subject laughs at himself.

My favourite, *The Non-conforming Non-conformist*, is about how Geoffrey, as an adolescent in the 1950s, loses an over-literal faith as a member of the Sutton Methodist Youth Club and how he finds – or rather tries to find – girls.

I shall give four excerpts; the first to show you how the play starts:

RUMBUSTIOUS INTRODUCTION ON THE CHAPEL HARMONIUM

GEOFFREY: (NARRATING) I was first taken to church when I was six years old.

THE CONGREGATION START SINGING A ROUSING EVANGELICAL HYMN. TAKE DOWN BEHIND.

GEOFFREY: Our family had its own pew. My grand-father sat with formidable dignity at the first place just by the aisle; next to him, more relaxed, came my father. Then my mother, my elder brother, John and finally me. I thought I behaved rather well in church, but nobody else shared this view. Complaints started with my grandfather and made their way along the pew.

BRING UP HYMN AGAIN

GRANDFATHER: Tell Geoffrey not to fidget so much.

FATHER: Oh yes. Claire, tell Geoffrey to behave him-self.

MOTHER: Yes dear. John, would you ask Geoffrey to try and sit still. It's not for much longer.

JOHN: Okay. (Loud whisper) Geoff!

YOUNG GEOFF: Yes?

JOHN: Shut up mucking around.

YOUNG GEOFF: I'm not doing anything.

JOHN: Shut up!

SWELL HYMN AND FADE

The play continues with Geoffrey frequently confused by religion. Even those of us who have not had a formal religious upbringing will recognise the wonderful confusions that grown ups can lead children into. Geoffrey Parkinson had the innocence to take such matters literally at the time, and the talent, later in life, to distil such experiences in his writing. For example, on one occasion his mother explained how they did not touch fermented liquor in their family and his father explained how many homes had been ruined by drink.

YOUNG GEOFF: Why did Jesus turn water into wine then?

MOTHER: Oh, I'm sure it wasn't real wine, Geoffrey. It couldn't have been fermented. I would have thought it was more like fruit juice. Wouldn't you, Will?

FATHER: I think it was real wine, Claire. But of course we have to bear in mind one very important fact. Jesus lived in the Middle East.

MOTHER: I don't quite follow you, Will. Surely alcóhol is evil wherever it's found.

FATHER: It's very different if you live in the Middle East, Claire. (With finality) Very different.

Geoffrey asks Dick, the boy down the road, what the Middle East is, and is told it is where people wear hardly any clothes and where they sit on nails.

Geoffrey's religious education is further confused when his brother John warns him of the terrible danger of worshipping graven images, that could for example even be plasticine models. Geoffrey is not terribly worried, because he has never been tempted to worship plasticine. At the age of six he is more interested in looking at little girls' willies and has vague qualms of conscience that this might be evil. Furthermore John goes on to point out that Geoffrey is in great danger, because he has used the word 'blimey'. This means he has asked God to blind him. Young Geoffrey tries desperately to say the word backwards, to undo the harm: 'Yemilb! Yemilb!'

However, I think he is at his funniest and most poignant when he has to join the youth club, where he first notices girls.

GEOFFREY: I remember that around that time, I'd just read Emily Brontë's 'Wuthering Heights'. I also went to see Laurence Olivier as Heathcliff and Merle Oberon as Cathy in the film at the local Odeon. What a film that was and what an effect it was to have.

EXCERPT FROM THE FILM'S ORIGINAL SOUND-TRACK: VOICES AND SWEET MUSIC

LAURENCE   Why isn't there the smell of heather in your
OLIVIER as   hair?
HEATHCLIFF:

MERLE OBERON   Oh, Heathcliff, why won't you let me come
as CATHY: near you? You're not black and horrible as they all think. You're full of pain. I can make you happy. Let me try. You won't regret it. I'll be your slave. I can bring life back to you.

OLIVIER: Why are your eyes always empty?

GRADUALLY LOSE THE FILM SOUND-TRACK BACK BEHIND GEOFFREY'S NARRATION.

GEOFFREY: (NARRATING) Sitting in the front stalls and asorbing all the high drama, an idea occurred to me. Now although I didn't feel I stood a dog's chance of attracting any girls on my own merits, it seemed possible, just possible, that if I could present myself to them as an imitation of Heathcliff, even as an imitation of Laurence Olivier, I might possibly make some sort of headway. At nights in my bedroom I tried, not very successfully, to imitate his beautiful, carefully delineated voice.

SCENE: GEOFFREY'S BEDROOM

GEOFFREY: (ALOUD) Your hair smells of the heather, Cathy. No. Your hair! – (BUT HIS VOICE TURNS INTO A SQUAWK) Your hair – (STILL NOT CONVINCED) Oh blast! (PAUSE) Your hair smells . . . that's better. Your hair smells of the heather. (NARRATING) When I tried the Heathcliff touch with the dumpy little blonde girl at the youth club, the result was slightly embarrassing.

SCENE: YOUTH CLUB

GEOFFREY: (OLIVIER IMITATION) Can I get you a cup of coffee, Mary?

MARY: I don't mind.

GEOFFREY: You like coffee, Mary?

MARY: Are you feeling all right?

GEOFFREY: Feeling all right, Mary?

MARY: Have you got a cold or something?

GEOFFREY: No. Why?

MARY: You sound different.

As director of the play I managed to lay my hands on a few minutes of the original sound-track of the film and we were able to let the listener compare Laurence Olivier's performance with Geoffrey's attempt to model himself on it. Geoffrey Beevers as Geoffrey Parkinson brought a superbly informed naiveté to the role.

During a visit to a production of *La Bohème*, Geoffrey then falls in love with Sybil, another girl from the youth club. He becomes a fervent, if somewhat misinformed, disciple of Freud and begins to drift away from the Chapel. Years later he receives a letter from the minister.

MINISTER: My dear Geoffrey, We have been looking through the list of Church members and notice that you have long since ceased to make a regular attendance. This is a great sadness, not only to us, but also, I am sure, to your dear mother and father. With the greatest reluctance, we have therefore decided that your name must be removed from the membership roll. I hope and pray that one day it may be joyfully reinstated. Yours sincerely, Frederick Whitfield Liggett. PS God bless you, my boy.

There are two things that I particularly love about this play:

1. There are many plays about lapsed faith in which playwrights tend to attack, or to be embittered by, their childhood faith. They tend neither to offer a positive alternative nor to suggest that there is more than one side to the question. Very often the reason for writing is a form of personal catharsis and therapy, but, in my opinion, many of these plays do very little to inform or to heal the listener. Geoffrey Parkinson's play is more objective. It is redeemed by compassion and affection, as well as by acute observation and a lovely sense of humour, that is directed as much at himself as at anybody else. In writing, as in real life, one needs these qualities to get at the truth of a character.

2. The humour has a slow burn to it. It only occasionally makes us laugh out loud, but it keeps a grin on our faces. It is based on recognition. We may think to ourselves: 'Oh yes, yes, I know that situation. I have been there and seen that, but I never quite realised before how enlightening and how funny such an everyday situation could be.' As Henry Fielding opines in his preface to *Joseph Andrews*: 'Life everywhere furnishes an accurate observer with the ridiculous.'

LOOKING AT SITUATION COMEDY

The Non-conforming Non-conformist could be said to be a comedy of character. There are some excellent radio comedies where it is the situation even more than the characters that make us chortle.

One such is *Crisp And Even Brightly* by Alick Rowe (although the characters too are hilarious at times). It purports to be the true story of Good King Wenceslaus. It won the Sony Comedy Award and ten years later, Miles Kington, one of the judges, still chortled at the memory of it.

This, thematically, was one of a series of plays. The first, *Operation Lightning Pegasus*, purported to be the true story of the siege of Troy and of the wooden horse, which was really the result of a monumental military cock-up by upper class twits on both sides. Achilles was a closet homosexual with a fatal taste in elegant sandals.

The second was called *Odysseus On An Iceberg*. Odysseus was a rotten navigator. He kept taking wrong turns and that's why he landed up on an iceberg and took 20 years to get home. Penelope wasn't worried. She loved having so many suitors.

Both these plays were subsequently given stage performances by many schools. Comedy can be a very effective means of education.

Crisp And Even Brightly points out the many absurdities and anomalies within the Christmas carol of Good King Wenceslaus. I often use the following scene from the play as an exercise when I am working with students on radio acting. It provides an explanation as to how the carol came to be composed.

(SCENE 11. KITCHEN. FX: AN ALARM BELL TOLLS. SMALL CROWD GATHERS.)

LUDMILLA (THE QUEEN MOTHER): Is everybody here and will somebody have that bell silenced? Is everybody here?

(FX: MASSIVE BANGING OF SAUCEPAN WITH SPOON)

CRONE: Quiet. A bit of quiet in my kitchen. (SILENCE) I should think so.

LUDMILLA:	Thank you, Crone. Vlad? Good. Otto and Sigmund. Spy? Good. Listen. We have a crisis. Listen. The king is nowhere to be found and there is a page missing.
CRONE:	Isn't that just typical.
LUDMILLA:	What?
CRONE:	Always the same; just when it gets exciting. Just as you get to the best bit of the book. Just when you are getting to know –
LUDMILLA:	(Over-riding) We are here to discover where he may have gone and what must be done; remembering of course that security is notoriously lax during the Christmas period and that Slavnik agents are known to be at hand. Speak.

(THIS SECTION SHOULD MOVE VERY FAST)

OTTO:	We saw him, Lady, up at his window.
SIGMUND:	This evening, early on.
LUDMILLA:	What were the conditions?
OTTO:	Snow lying, Lady.
SIGMUND:	Deep snow.
OTTO:	Levelled and honed by the wind and the frost.
SIGMUND:	Terrible frost, Lady.
OTTO:	Cruel.
LUDMILLA:	Suspicious circumstances?
SIGMUND:	A poor man, Lady, hanging about.

OTTO: Said he was looking for wood.

SIGMUND: Then the King called down for young Mark. That's his page.

CRONE: Mark the page? Nasty habit.

LUDMILLA: Thank you, Crone.

OTTO: Only the boy was down with us, you see, Lady.

HARRY THE SPY: That's right. If you remember, up he came to the room, while we were there. After we'd gone the King ordered him to the window and pointed out this so-called-though-now-infinitely-suspicious poor man.

CRONE: Oh, no. 'Peasant' he said he was.

SIGMUND: Who said who said who was?

CRONE: The boy said the King said the poor man was.

VLADIMIR: Certainly, Lady Ludmilla, it was upon the basis that the poor man was a positive peasant that I calculated the relevant provisions.

HARRY: Anyway, the King asked the boy who this poor man or peasant was and where he was from, what sort of house he had.

LUDMILLA: But how do you know all this?

HARRY: Listened through the key hole. That's my job. I'm a spy.

OTTO: The pageboy – he'd be able to give all this information because he'd heard us question the man.

SIGMUND: Yes. Lives just over three miles away.

OTTO: Foot of the forest.

SIGMUND: Just follow the fence.

OTTO: Along to St Agnes' Fountain.

EVERYBODY: Where?

LUDMILLA: Anyway.

VLADIMIR: Anyway – flesh, wine and logs were required: pine logs.

CRONE: They were going to deliver it all and be back in time for dinner.

OTTO: Wait a minute –

SIGMUND: The walking woodpile?

OTTO: Right.

SIGMUND: We saw them leave the palace, Lady. Just when the blizzard was starting up.

LUDMILLA: So what we have so far is this:

(THE BREAK-NECK PACE SLOWS DOWN NOW. AS THE NARRATIVE IS TOLD IN THE PALACE, THE MUSIC OF THE CAROL SHOULD CREEP IN BEHIND THE WORDS)

'Good King Wenceslaus looked out, on the feast of Stephen, when the snow lay round about, deep and crisp and even. Brightly shone the moon that night – though the frost was cruel – when a poor man came in sight, gathering winter fuel.'

CRONE: Fuel?

VLADIMIR: Fuel.

HARRY: 'Hither, page, and stand by me, if thou knowest it telling: yonder peasant who is he? Where and what his dwelling?'

OTTO: 'Sire, he lives a good league hence –'

SIGMUND: 'Underneath the mountain. Hard against the forest fence –'

OTTO: 'By St Agnes' Fountain.'

CRONE: Where?

VLADIMIR: 'Bring me flesh and bring me wine. Bring me pine-logs hither. Thou and I shall see him dine e'er we dine together.'

OTTO: 'Page –'

SIGMUND: 'And Monarch –'

OTTO: 'Forth they went;'

OTTO/SIGMUND: 'Forth they went together;'

ALL: 'Through the rude wind's wild lament –'

(STOP MUSIC)

LUDMILLA: 'And the bitter weather'. Yes I see. Guards!

OTTO/SIGMUND: Yes, Lady?

LUDMILLA: Spy?

HARRY: Yes, Lady?

LUDMILLA: After them. We shall await further reports. (PAUSE) Who was carrying this several hundred-weight of fatuous good will?

OTTO:	The boy.
LUDMILLA:	As I thought. And who was leading the way?
SIGMUND:	The King.
LUDMILLA:	Precisely. They won't have gone far.

Alick Rowe demonstrates an impressive ability to keep the jokes and the invention pouring out page after page, for 75 minutes. On the day *Crisp And Even Brightly* was broadcast, a friend driving up the M1 told me how many other drivers he had seen, roaring with laughter, and thus he knew who else was listening.

I also still laugh whenever I hear Peter Tinniswood's series of plays about the West Country poacher and philosopher, Winston Heyballs. This excerpt is about whether the middle class family Winston has adopted is going to move yet again. It is an inspired and outrageous, politically incorrect diatribe. It is so original, poetic and funny, that he gets away with it, with flying colours.

FATHER:	I've decided, Nancy.
NANCY:	What have you decided, Father?
FATHER:	To move house.
NANCY:	Oh my God!
FATHER:	It's the wanderlust, you see, Old Boy.
NANCY:	Wanderlust?
FATHER:	Yes. Itchy pants. A slow deep yearning in the creaking cockles of the heart. A constant, throbbing ache in the nether regions of the popping crease. I want to be off on my travels again, Nancy. I want to experience new sights, new sounds, new smells.

I want to be stimulated and excited and enchanted and have my soul completely refurbished.

NANCY: Father, I'm not going to live in Harrogate again and that is that!

FATHER: The screech of monkeys and the grunt of tiger.
Temple gongs crooning soft in forests thick with teak.
Pantiles blistering with summer sun in the Auvergne.
The salt spit of winter barges on the Zuider Zee.
(PAUSE)
Oh my God, I could murder an Eccles cake.

NANCY: What!?

FATHER: Well this country's going to the dogs, Nancy.
You can't get a decent Eccles cake for love nor money these days.
In my youth, in the days of my prime, England was bursting at the seams with Eccles cakes; succulent, sticky, oozing with sensuous spices from the Orient.
And then the bloody Nips came along and ruined it all.

NANCY: What?

FATHER: The Nips, Old Boy, the Japs.
Fearful little slant-eyed stinkers, hell-bent on destroying our planet.
Killing all the dolphins, massacring the whales, poisoning the air we breathe with their ghastly gibbering motor bikes.
What's wrong with Norton and A.G.S and Messerschmitts? Bloody Nips!
If I had a medium sized tooth pick handy, I'd kebab the whole lot of them, string 'em up as food for the tom tits.
I can't stand Gregorian chant either.

NANCY: What?

FATHER: And Woman's Hour has gone to the dogs too!
           Well what do I care about the menstrual problems
           of one parent lesbian bus conductors?

NANCY: Father, I'm not quite clear what you're getting at.

FATHER: Well, what I'm getting at, Old Boy, is quite simple.
           I don't want to live in England any more.

Gillian Reynolds, the courageous and perceptive critic, wrote of
Visiting Julia, another Peter Tinniswood series: 'There it is, clear
as a bell, the individual voice of a writer, who knows his craft,
loves his audience, makes brilliant, memorable characters, who
unfailingly transform big fears and little failings into laughter.'
Dear reader, try and find your own, original voice in this way.

7

Writing Short Stories, Dramatisations and *The Archers*

SHORT STORY WRITING

Writing short stories is simpler – but not necessarily easier – than writing plays and features.

The short story writer will often, in the first half of the story, endeavour to keep the reader in a state of suspended animation. The writer may often only reveal a mood, a mystery, a setting or a character. He may be content to tantalise the reader, knowing that the reader will read on – or even skip forward – to find out what is going to happen. Readers will know that in the end they should be rewarded with a satisfying twist or resolution.

A classic short story in this genre is *Taste* by Roald Dahl.

In the first short paragraph the author sets the scene, a smart dinner party in the 1960s. In the second he introduces the famous guest, Richard Pratt, a connoisseur of fine food and wine. The scene is observed by the old family retainer as well as by the reader. Pratt refers to wines as if they were people: 'A rather shy wine, but quite clever'. His wealthy host Mike is in the habit of betting him a case of the wine in question, that he cannot identify it. This evening, however, Richard appears to be more interested in drooling over Mike's nubile 18 year-old daughter. So Mike ups the odds. He is a wealthy man and slowly the stake is increased, until he bets Richard anything he likes to name, that he cannot identify the claret. The tension mounts and finally Richard names his price: 'Your daughter in marriage'. Mike accepts: Richard cannot possibly guess such an obscure vineyard. You can imagine Mike's wife's and daughter's reactions. Richard narrows the claret down to a Médoc, to a St Julien, to the Beychevelle District: 'possibly a Talbot, no – no – a smaller château – a Branaire-Ducru'. And he's won the nubile daughter!

The story-telling is so compelling, the characterisation so accurate that the reader suspends disbelief. And the twist? The old family retainer has spotted him going into the library, where Mike had left the wine to *chambré* before dinner.

The ending comes as a surprise, but when one thinks about it afterwards, both in terms of situation and of character, it was inevitable. This makes for a powerful and satisfying short story.

WRITING FOR READING ALOUD

I asked my friend the poet, short story writer and playwright, Ted Walker, for his view on the difference between a short story read silently and one read aloud. He started by replying, that as a 'Writer of Short Stories for Radio' he was a complete fraud, that he never once sat down to write a story specially for broadcasting. However, what he went on to say demonstrated that as a poet he had been addressing the question of writing to be read aloud for most of his working life. Ted possesses that endearing combination of qualities often found in excellent writers: humility and intelligence.

He wrote: 'I think my work may have had some success on air, because I'm a painter *manqué*. When I was a kid, nobody taught me to draw. I grew into manhood terrified (whenever I tried, abysmally, to paint) lest somebody look over my shoulder. I couldn't do it. But then, luckily, my Dad sent me (when I was 10) to learn French with a Monsieur Jupp – who became Herr Jupp when we began to play-act in German and Signor Jupp when, playing the part of a waiter, he started serving invisible pasta. I became a linguist. I was obsessed, thoroughly entranced, with words; and English words became the best materials for visual communication that I had. The old cliché about 'painting with words' became true for me.

'There's really nothing complicated, I guess, about certain kinds of successful writing for radio. Words *do* make pictures in the listener's head. (There's a truism for you! But it had better be said yet again, lest the obvious gets lost in theoreticising.) It so happens that my kind of picture-making sometimes works equally well when the words are listened to rather than looked at on the page.

'It must be stressed however that my technique is an intensely *literary* one. I know what I'm up to, while hoping that my reader/listener doesn't. Words don't just *mean* this or that: they *embody* with the sounds they make. The pictures one creates of an action should catch, with the style of its expression, the very rhythm of what's going on. If you get the rhythm right, the listener or reader, willy-nilly finds himself – his limbs, his head, whatever – joining in. In his imagination he stumbles, or strides out, or hops on one leg. Leslie Norris wrote a poem in which the simple words, "I wound down the window" occur. Try it aloud: "I wound down the window". See? One turn for "wound" and another for "down"; the window by now is about three-quarters open, right? And with the arrival of "window" you've got the glass fully down. The feel of this is all but totally absent from plain old: "I opened the window". (Of course, you can't get this effect now that we've got electrically operated windows!)

'Words on the page can be gone over at the reader's leisure, again and again. On radio, you have to get through to the listener *premier coup*. So your story had better not have too complex a narrative thread nor too complicated a plot. A sense of place has to be evoked (the other senses have a vital part to play here: it's not just the eyes that "see"). Characters must speak – and (how obvious!) speak *in character*. Possibly more important than *action* is description of what's going on simultaneously with the action. (Smoke coming out of a remote cottage chimney somehow gives more point to the murder that's going on in the kitchen.) Accuracy of detail is vital. You never use words like "tree" or "car"; say "poplar" or "Rolls".'

Ted went on to say, 'I think every one of my radio dramas was adapted from one of my *New Yorker* short stories. Again, any success I might have had with radio is down to my particular way of seeing the world. My poetry has the same visual/audio qualities. In a poem in which I remember when my grandfather died, and I had an asthma attack when I was told he was dead, and he had not long since told me that it wasn't yet time to have a bonfire, I had the asthma attack – alluded to – actually enacted with the line:

"His fire shot higher than hollyhocks".

'All those aitches, you see, catch the short breaths of asthma. This is to show how the rabbit is stowed in the top hat. I swear you to secrecy!' Ted has graciously allowed me to lift the veil, so that writer may speak to writer within the pages of this book.

WRITING DRAMATISATIONS

The classic serial remains one of the BBC's most successful and long-standing slots and the art of dramatising novels is alive and well. Generally only experienced playwrights will be invited to undertake the task, as experience of how radio drama works and engages the listener is essential. It is often necessary to take considerable liberties with the structure of a novel, in order to convey the essence of the work to the listener in an engaging and compelling manner. The experience of reading, where one can close or open a book or go back or skim forward, is very different from that of listening to the continuum of a radio play. Dramatists cannot afford to be as discursive as novelists.

Also the beginning of a dramatisation is crucial. While one can feel oneself slowly into a novel, this cannot be the case with a dramatisation.

One of the first English novels, *Joseph Andrews* by Henry Fielding, begins: 'It is a trite but true observation, that examples work more forcibly on the mind than precepts: and if this be just in what is odious and blameable, it is more strongly so in what is amiable and praiseworthy.' It is assumed by the author that the reader has all the time in the world to share his reflection, before getting caught up in the story. The dramatisation on the other hand needs either to project the listener into an involving story or at least to entertain him from the outset.

In his dramatisation of *Joseph Andrews*, John Scotney decided to give us some of Fielding's more entertaining philosophising on the subject of chastity, before plunging us into the story. This allowed us to participate in the authorial voice, an important element in this novel, and to gain something of the flavour of the period.

Here is the beginning:

(TECHNICAL NOTE: THE PRODUCTION SHOULD BE SEAMLESS. THEREFORE THE SCENES SIMPLY INDICATE POSSIBLE RECORDING BREAKS. OFTEN FX AND BACKGROUND FROM A PREVIOUS SCENE WILL TUCK UNDER SPEECH FROM A FOLLOWING SCENE)

ANNOUNCER: 'Joseph Andrews' by Henry Fielding, dramatised in four episodes by John Scotney.

(MUSIC: A LIVELY AND HUMOROUS EIGHTEENTH
CENTURY PASTICHE)

FIELDING   The first part, which treats of the death of
(AS NARRATOR):   Sir Thomas Booby, with the affectionate
                  and mournful behaviour of his widow and
                  the great chastity of Joseph.

1st ACTRESS: (Fervently respectful) Chastity!

2nd ACTRESS: (Ditto) Chastity!

PARSON ADAMS: (Ditto) Ah yes, chastity!

SEVERAL OTHER   (Mocking) What!
LADIES WITH
LADY BOOBY:

FIELDING: Nay, is not male chastity as becoming to the
                  human species as female? Yet the character
                  of a chaste *man* is a thing few authors
                  among the moderns have seen fit to dwell
                  upon.

1st ACTRESS: Whilst female chastity is everywhere to be
                  found, at least in the book shops.

2nd ACTRESS: (Catty) Who has not heard of the cele-
                  brated chastity of sweet, dear, pretty
                  Pamela Andrews?

ACTOR: So admirably recorded by Mr Samuel
                  Richardson in his 'Pamela'.

2nd ACTRESS: (Over-sweetly) Or – 'Virtue Rewarded.'

(NEXT FEW SPEECHES ARE HYPOCRITICALLY
PRURIENT)

1st ACTRESS: Pamela, a pretty fifteen year old servant
                  girl, artlessly sets down how she virtuously
                  resisted all manner of lewd and lustful

assaults by her master – including an attempted rape,

2nd ACTOR: Which she describes in some detail.

1st ACTRESS: Until defeated at last by her chastity, her master offered her the joy of becoming his wife.

2nd ACTRESS: And so was able legitimately to enjoy those attentions,
(LADIES BEGIN TO LAUGH)
he had so often attempted to enforce on her in vain.

1st ACTOR: Such a theme is the soul of religion, good breeding (Unctuous) and morality in our present age; and the pulpit as well as the coffee house has resounded with Pamela's praise.

2nd ACTOR: But what of her brother?

JOSEPH: Mr *Joseph* Andrews, who by keeping his sister's virtues ever before his eyes,

ADAMS: and attending to the wise advice of the Reverend Mr Abraham Adams,

JOSEPH: was also able to preserve *his* chastity in the face of as many and as great temptations as were placed before his sister.

2nd ACTRESS: Who has heard of him?

(MUSIC OUT, RATHER SHARPLY)

1st ACTRESS: Who among those thousands to whom the name '*Pamela* Andrews' is now so familiar, has heard of *Joseph* Andrews?

1st ACTOR:	To correct the which omission we now present before the public the authentic:

(A COMIC CHORD OR TWO OF MUSIC)

FIELDING:	HISTORY OF THE ADVENTURES OF JOSEPH ANDREWS AND HIS FRIEND, MR ABRAHAM ADAMS, as faithfully recorded by your servant, Mr Henry Fielding, Gent.

(UNDER THE END OF PREVIOUS SPEECH ESTABLISH THE JOYFUL PEALING OF ENGLISH CHURCH BELLS AND RUSTICS MURMURING 'YOUR HONOUR')

FIELDING:	Our history opens in the year of Grace, 1737, upon a Sunday morning in summer (ADD BIRDSONG) as Parson Adams walks through the churchyard, receiving the bows and salutations of his flock –

And so the play has started and the story proper may now begin. Several points have been established in this opening passage:

1. John Scotney was able to introduce the full title and thus something of the 18th century flavour of the novel without its seeming longeur.

2. We are informed that the novel was intended as a satire upon the recently published, 'first' English novel, *Pamela* by Samuel Richardson.

3. The author, Henry Fielding, will be the narrator.

4. However, he will share this function with his main characters, who will often introduce and describe themselves (as do Joseph and Adams and a voice we may later recognise as Lady Booby's). This convention seemed very much to belong to Fielding's style of making asides.

5. The opening scene has been introduced.

There is not space here to take you through this dramatisation of *Joseph Andrews* step by step. However, let me give you some general pointers. Apart from accomplishing the vitally important opening, the dramatiser will need to compile a thorough synopsis of the plot. He can then break the novel down into episodes. Classic serial episodes are normally about 57 minutes long and there are also usually some slots for modern novels dramatised in 27-minute episodes.

Compelling 'cliff-hangers' will help persuade the listeners to make a date with future episodes. However, the dramatiser should not assume that the listener will have heard previous episodes and thus from the second episode on 'action so far' should be economically and entertainingly contained in the beginning of each episode.

Finally the writer should then break each episode down into a variety of scenes to keep the listener as enthralled as possible.

Strangely enough the next section on *The Archers* might also give some help in this respect.

SCRIPT WRITING FOR *THE ARCHERS*

I am firmly of the opinion that there is only room for one soap opera on national radio. The BBC has had a spate of managers who have asked drama producers, 'Where are the *Eastenders*, the *Casualty*s of radio?' These managers have mostly come from television and have not fully grasped how differently radio works. It can take a dedicated listener several years to identify with the characters in a radio soap opera, to create the settings in their imaginations, to feel that an 'Ambridge' is part of their daily lives.

The Archers is over 50 years old and had already made a national impact when Grace Archer was burnt to death on the night that ITV was launched. Today there is a basic team of ten writers who, with the guidance of the editor and the producers, keep the stories flowing year after year.

Should you want to become one of these writers, you should send off to BBC Pebble Mill (Birmingham B5 7QQ) for 'The Archers Pack.' Following the brief therein, you can write an episode on spec. If you surmount this hurdle and are considered promising, you will be invited to a mock script conference. After this you will be sent away to write a synopsis for a week's storylines. 'This is the real killer,' says Caroline Harrington, one of the writing team. Each week there are six episodes of twelve and a half minutes each and each episode should have a maximum of five scenes. Each episode should have about seven characters and the continuities of the major (three-month stories) and minor stories (of about a month) need to be kept going. One of your problems is that, unlike TV soap opera, characters rarely leave. Thus death and divorce can very rarely be part of the plot-lines. Listen for yourself and note down what the major and minor stories are, running through each episode over a week or more.

If you are fortunate enough to be invited on to the team, you will often be briefed as to which actors are going to be available. The actors are not under contract and may be lured away by more financially or artistically rewarding work in television or the theatre. You will be given a list of forthcoming events, eg the Queen's 60th wedding anniversary, to incorporate into your week's episodes. You will also probably be leant on by the agricultural adviser, to make sure you are up to date with developments in farming. Incidentally modern farming poses an interesting problem for dramatists as most of it is a lonely process and lengthy internal monologues on tractors are not exactly *The Archers* style.

As long as you do not lose your original voice or vision, your vocation, this can be a very good training for other forms of radio writing.

WRITING FOR *STATION ROAD*

Since January 1999 BBC Radio Wales have been broadcasting their soap every weekday morning. The producer writes:

Set in the fictional town Bryncoed, it is a more urban drama than *The Archers*. If you wish to write for this lively drama, I suggest you listen to it. You can get BBC Radio Wales on a Sky Digital satellite receiver, channel 928, anywhere in Europe, or you could try tuning to 882 MW (which does reach some strange parts of the country, especially for some reason in the car). Then send us a sample of your work. This could be a piece for television, radio or theatre. If the producer likes it, he will send you the 'Writers' Guidelines' for the show and invite you to a script meeting. You will be expected to write a test synopsis and a week's worth of scripts. The synopsis is crucial to the process of writing and producing *Station Road*. It will show how well you know the world and its characters, before you've put any words in their mouths. Radio Wales has a smaller budget than Radio 4. You can only cast five characters per episode or 25 across the week, and a minimum of six scenes per episode are required.

Your presence is only required for the one-day script meeting. The delivery of your synopsis and scripts can be done electronically and feedback and re-writes are given over the phone. Being on line is worthwhile as this can give you an extra day writing, so don't be put off if you don't live in the Principality.

WESTWAY

Just as *The Archers* was instituted under the guise of entertainment to relay information to farmers and help with our agricultural recovery after the Second World War, so the BBC World Service is advising on radio soap operas to help solve economic and social problems in Russia (in which Tony Blair made a guest appearance as himself), Romania, Albania and Afghanistan, and is planning one in Vietnam. BBC World Service also has its own English soap with the largest radio drama audience in the world. If you are a night owl listen to *Westway* and, if you want to write for it, approach one of the producers.

8

Writing and Compiling a Radio Feature

DEFINING A RADIO FEATURE

The earliest radio drama, with a few exceptions, consisted of stage plays adapted for radio. Before the war in Manchester and Bristol, G D Bridson and Francis Dillon were compiling unscripted recordings of local speech to make pure radio features. In 1945 the Features Department moved to London, where producers experimented with the medium to create works of art specially written for radio. Such were Dylan Thomas' *Under Milkwood* and Louis MacNiece's *The Dark Tower*. However, by the 1960s most new ideas and scripts submitted to BBC Radio were specifically written for radio in the first place.

Today the term 'feature' has come to mean anything from a five minute report on the chicken industry, recorded on location, to an open ended Dominican Debate on the Existence of God on Radio 3. For the purpose of this chapter I shall take it to mean a creative piece of writing and production, where the elements do not consist solely of scripted drama as we traditionally understand them. Very often, as in the form called 'drama documentary' or 'faction', they will be constructed out of fact, rather than out of fiction.

As in previous chapters, I can best illustrate this from my own productions, not because they are better than others, but simply because I know the intentions that inform them and how they were put together.

One of my happier and productive working relationships in the field of features has been with the writer Mike Walker. He is prolific of ideas and of fresh approaches and I have tried in turn to be his guide, philosopher and friend, to help him realise what I think will work splendidly and to modify and clarify what might be confusing or alienating to the listener. As I shall explain in the next chapter I think the producer has as much as possible to put himself in the place of the listener.

WRITING HISTORICAL FEATURES

One of our first joint ventures was a feature about Chief Sitting Bull of the Sioux Indians, called *A Warrior I Have Been*. Mike was particularly interested in exploring the different mindsets and cultural values of the Red Indians and of the White Americans in the 19th century. He pointed out to me how much more formal and prepared was the speech of the Indians. He suggested that their lines should be scripted, in the form of blank verse, containing a measured authority. They would have a sense of the importance of the spoken word, the holiness of the oral tradition, common to mankind before the invention of printing and of the media. They might speak in the considered way that one has to when speaking through an interpreter. To contrast with this he suggested that we should give fact sheets to the actors portraying White soldiers, upon which they should improvise. If they stumbled, searched for words and were garbled in their delivery, this would be appropriate. Not only were many of them not very well educated, but perhaps in their heart of hearts they were uneasy at their treatment of the Indians and this unease might betray itself in incoherence.

The listener would not know that we had prepared the feature in this way, but if we had got it right the result, the production would ring true.

Here are two examples of what I mean. The first is a transcript of a White official:

My name's Macloughlin, Injun agent at Standin' Rock. Now, I reckon I'm a reasonable man, but (*Sighs*) I just can't understand why Sitting Bull won't toe the godamned line just like most of the other Injuns on the reservation. I mean, well let's face it now the days of the Injun are over. When Sitting Bull surrendered, came back from Canada that was it. Trouble is our Sitting Bull isn't like those Injuns who co-operated or let me set 'em up as chiefs or members of the Injun police. Not on your life. When there's trouble you can bet he's in on it.

How different is the prepared and measured language of one of the Indians:

Listen.

I, Wanbli Sapa, Black Eagle, was there.

It was before dawn.

Sitting Bull, Tatanka Yotanka, was sleeping in his cabin.

The door was kicked open and the police came in.

They said, they'd come to arrest him.

They said, that they were holding him.

They said, that if he resisted them, he would be killed where
    he was.

He said, 'Yes.'

He had to dress and they helped him, trying to be quick
    before any others should come and interrupt their work.

They were clumsy.

They pushed him through the door.

He was not properly dressed.

His dignity was hurt to be seen by the people in this way.

But he was not afraid.

The police were afraid.

Notice how many pictures are created by the Indian's speech. The agent's speech, on the other hand, conveys mainly his subjective emotions.

Still on the subject of one culture clashing with another, Mike Walker was pretty shrewd in 1979. He asked me whether I knew that 1988 would be the bicentenary of the first white settlement of Australia. He outlined a possible drama documentary series of 13 one-hour programmes, taking us from the first records of Aborigine culture up to the bicentenary ceremonies in 1988. We came to christen the series 'The Long March of Every Oz'.

Thirteen hours may seem ample, but when you have the entire history of a nation to cover, it can seem limiting. Mike suggested that we should paint a rich historical tapestry of activities and events with a contemporary commentator as guide. Thus an Australian version of a Michael Palin or Tony Robinson as a time traveller, strolling through the action, would point out the convicts building the first settlement, the early gold diggers in Melbourne buying their provisions and their whores or a Victorian lady settler in the outback playing an upright piano just imported from Liverpool.

Against this background we should have comment from some of Australia's leading historians of contrasting political persuasions and readings from source material such as journals, letters home, transcripts of trials, bills of lading, etc.

Then with careful multi-tracking and sound balance, so that we did not confuse the listener with too much complexity of sound, we should weave in and out of a background of work songs, military orders, drunken brawls, the herding of cattle, copper mining a kilometre below ground at Mount Isa, etc. Most of our backgrounds were recorded on location, while our foregrounds were recorded mostly in the studio.

This was the basic technique, though with many variations and with telling quieter sequences. It required much time spent in post production.

The earlier episodes were recorded almost entirely in the UK and the later ones in Australia. The break point between the two was made by a fairly arbitrary decision on our part as to when, where and how the Australian accent evolved from an amalgam of British and Irish accents. Some joke that it started because the Australians kept their mouths half closed so the flies wouldn't get in. Others say the upward inflexion at the end of a sentence is due to their coming from a government run country, where people are naturally deferential. However, several historians suggested that the accent developed from such bush rangers, outlaws and outback 'boyos' as Ned Kelly in the 1880s. Young rebels, in this case the poor Irish versus the English settlers, might well have developed their own slang and intonation as a badge of identity. We settled for this last theory. It made a nice watershed in the historical, dramatic narrative.

Another challenging problem in such a series is that of mixing sources, which are read by actors, with excerpts from recorded interviews. Actors by contrast will often sound 'performed' and the interviewees more real. To overcome this we often adopted a similar technique to that which we used for the White Americans in *A Warrior I Have Been*. We gave fact sheets or resumés to the actors and asked them to rephrase them in their own words.

I should like to take you through part of the last episode of the series, to demonstrate how we attempted to overcome some of the problems we encountered. It consisted mostly, but no means entirely, of 'vox-pop'. It was entitled *Lucky Country*? The irony of the question mark was intended.

HANDLING 'VOX-POP' FEATURES

We wanted to contrast the poet's view of the quiet, timeless life of the bush with the business of the urban, 20th century; so we started with a poem:

BIRDS, CRICKETS, ETC: THE MUTED SOUNDS OF THE AUSTRALIAN BUSH AT MIDDAY.

ACTOR: Axe-fall, echo and silence. Noon day silence.
Two miles from here, it is the twentieth century:
cars on the bitumen, power lines vaulting the farms.
Here, with my axe, I am chopping into the stillness.
Axe-fall, echo and silence. I pause, roll tobacco,
twist a cigarette, lick it. All is still.

INTRODUCE PEACEFUL MUSIC

I lean on my axe. A crowd of fragrant leaves
hangs over me, moveless, pierced everywhere by
sky.

The poem continues and the peaceful music segues into the title music.

We talked long and hard about whether we should have the sound of the axe chopping into the wood. We finally decided against it. It is there in the poem. Radio is about providing an outline that the listener can fill in. As well as pictures the listeners can imagine sounds, smells and the feeling of things and they can be all the more perfect, all the more powerful and evocative for being imagined. Let us not interrupt the listener doing his work.

The bespoke music, however, composed by Elizabeth Parker, is introduced at the precise moment that it can most effectively intensify and prolong the pictures already forming in our mind.

May I suggest that as an exercise you attempt to analyse the different elements – scripted readings, interviews, actuality, etc. – that we had to record and assemble in this opening and in the following (abridged) excerpt. See if it tallies with the list I shall give at the end of the passage.

EPIC THEME MUSIC IS FADED DOWN

ANNOUNCER: Episode Thirteen: 'Lucky Country?' After the boom, multiculturalism and the search for new values.

SWELL MUSIC AND THEN FADE TO SILENCE

MANNING-
CLARKE:
(Historian)

I was very enthusiastic about Gough Whitlam, because he was one of those gifted men, who believed the labour movement could create a society, in which there was equality of opportunity, without spiritual popery, without conformism and without pandering to mediocrity.

START SONG: 'TIME FOR FREEDOM' IN BACK-GROUND. WEAVE IN AND OUT OF FOLLOWING SPEAKERS

WOMAN: I don't think deep down we actually believed it could happen.

MAN 1: A lot of people clearly felt it was time.

MAN 2: We had years and years of Conservative government under Menzies and he tried to do things for Australia in a hurry. He knew that the forces of reaction would get him out of power.

MAN 3: We were in a period of decline, brought about by the skilful manipulative moves of the new president of the trade union movement of Australia, Mr Robert James Lee Hawke. Inflation was on the rise.
Unemployment was rising. Liberals were hoisted and Gough's banner 'It's time' was all the go.

SWELL SONG 'TIME FOR FREEDOM' TO CONCLUSION AND MIX WITH ACTUALITY OF GOUGH WHITLAM'S SPEECH. USE THE CROWD'S SPONTANEOUS CHEERS TO WEAVE IN AND OUT OF HIS SPEECH AND OF VOX POP

WHITLAM: Men and women of Australia, there are moments in history when the whole fate and future of nations can be decided by a single decision. For Australia this is such a time.

CHEERS

MAN 4:   I was a fan of Whitlam. Whitlam embodied many of the things that Menzies had, funnily enough, this tall, leonine, silver-haired figure with fluent tongue and persuasive arguments. I suppose, people wanted to revere him in a similar fashion.

CHEERS

WHITLAM: We will abolish conscription forthwith.

CHEERS

NARRATOR: During their first few days in office Labour made sweeping changes.

WHITLAM: Not just because a volunteer army is a better army, but because it's intolerable that a free nation at peace and not under threat should cull by lottery the best of its youth to provide defence on the cheap.

CHEERS

HUMPHREY
MACQUEEN:
(Marxist
Historian)   These were people who believed that there was enough wealth in the country to do something for the poor and for Aborigines and that it was no longer necessary to despoil the environment in order to have enough dirt to sell to the Japanese.

WHITLAM: We will legislate to give the Aborigines land rights.

CHEERS

MACQUEEN: Questions like urban planning and the environment and the Arts entered into the political agenda.

WHITLAM: Australians are diminished while the Aborigines are denied their rightful place in this nation.

CHEERS

WOMAN 2:   The two most important things that happened early in the Whitlam period were freedom of education and withdrawal of troops from Vietnam.

WHITLAM: It's time for a new team, a new programme, a new drive for equality of opportunities. Time for a new vision of what we achieve in this generation for our nation.

CHEERS

MAN 5:   The Labour Government spent like drunken sailors. Government spending increased by seventy five percent. Wages exploded by over fifty percent.

MAN 6:   Prices went through the roof. When you think ten dollars and somebody comes along and says 'think a hundred', the whole spectrum of the community changes.

MAN 5:   Businesses went to the wall.

MACQUEEN: The people who attacked him were saying, 'There's too much governmental activity of every kind in every way.'

WHITLAM: We ought to be angry with a deep determined anger that a country as rich and skilled as ours should be producing so much inequality, so much poverty, so much that is shoddy and sub-standard.

> We ought to be angry with an unrelenting anger that our Aborigines have the world's highest infant mortality rate.

CLAPPING

> We ought to be angry on our children's behalf, at the mindless destruction of our national and historical heritage.

CHEERS

MACQUEEN: Australian intellectual life really came of age since the seventies with Patrick White's winning of the Nobel Prize, with Australians winning the Booker Prize, with the Australian film industry.

NARRATOR: Macdonald's opened their first take-away, wine boxes appeared, the Sydney Opera House was opened.

BLASTS AND WHOOPS OF SHIPS' SIRENS IN SYDNEY HARBOUR, VAST CROWD CHEERING, ACTUALITY FROM THE DAY OF THE OPENING.

GIRL: The Queen came to open it. It was really exciting. Everyone loved it. It was exciting for us and she came and did a tour. And all the schools were out in force and waved and she waved back – at me!

NARRATOR: It was a boom time, enhanced by the richness of the nation's mineral reserves. Nothing seemed impossible.

MACQUEEN: We could buy champagne and caviar till the cows came home and this kept pushing up the value of the dollar until by 1974 the Australian dollar was worth 1.44 American dollars. We were on the crest of the wave. We could travel around the world, everything was cheap. It was the bonanza years of selling off Australia.

SONG 'LADY SUNSHINE'

MAN 9:   Well, if it's good enough for Whitlam it's good enough for me, because it's the first decent, bloody government we've ever had for twenty-three years.

SWELL SONG AGAIN: 'LADY SUNSHINE, LET YOUR SUN SHINE ON ME'

I have quoted at length, because I should like to invite you to think not only about how this first 20 minutes of '*Lucky Country*?' works for the listener, but to examine how it was put together.

EXAMINING THE BUILDING BLOCKS OF A FEATURE

Assembling the foregoing was a complex and time-consuming process. Let's look at the different elements that go to make up the whole.

1. The scripted reading of the poem by an actor recorded in a BBC studio in Bristol, England.

2. Epic title music to give us the sense of scale of such a large island nation and of the sweep of history. The listener, hopefully, will have come to identify with this music over the previous twelve episodes.

3. The woman announcer, recorded in an ABC Studio in Sydney, who gives us the title and the theme of the episode. (The credits are left to the end.)

4. Interviews with two leading historians were recorded in studios in Canberra. Mike Walker prepared a series of questions for them, which we asked them to respond to as spontaneously, coherently and concisely as they could. One of the problems of putting together a feature of this nature is the amount of

repetition and meandering that one has to edit out. If you can brief the interviewee effectively and train him to contain your question within his answer, you can save hours of editing.

5. Vox-pop interviews edited to advance the story, to represent both sides of the political equation and to convey the excitement and hope at the election of Gough Whitlam in 1975. Probably the most strenuous part of the exercise was the days and days of gathering and then editing down to identifiable, meaningful and attractive sound-bites: literally hundreds of hours of interviews with ordinary Australians.

6. Other interviews were kindly provided from the archives of the Australian Broadcasting Company, as was the recording of Gough Whitlam's speech together with the recordings of crowds and ships' sirens from the opening of the Sydney Opera House.

7. Under the BBC's agreement with the Performing Rights Society we were able to use the songs 'It's Time' and 'Mr Sunshine'.

8. Wild track recordings (for dramatic license and technical interweaving) of crowds cheering and responding. As much as possible we used the authentic and actual responses to Whitlam's speech. Dramatically it was important, that these sounded spontaneous and heartfelt and that they conveyed the appropriate celebration and exuberance. Also there were background recordings of birdsong, etc from the BBC's and the ABC's recorded sound effects libraries.

9. Rather late in this episode we introduce the narrator to link speakers and to convey some necessary information. Some listeners may recognise him as our guide from previous episodes. Others may think he is just another vox pop interviewee. It does not matter. The same may be true of Humphrey MacQueen, the second historian.

So this was the raw material as it were. How did we plan the operation? Then how did we assemble and put together the material?

In the first place, Mike Walker produced a draft outline of our intentions and objectives and of the proposed structure of the programme. In this final episode, we knew that we wanted to convey as broad a spectrum of every aspect of Australian life and attitudes as possible from the accession of Whitlam in 1972 to the bicentenary in 1988.

We planned to use Les Murray's poem, *Noonday Axeman* to open and close the programme and to guide us from one part to another. We planned to convey the rise of Whitlam and the story of Cyclone Tracey in the first part; the sacking of Whitlam by Her Majesty's Governor General and a canter through descriptions of Australia's mineral resources, multiculturalism, religion, sport and crime in the second part; and to have the bicentennial celebrations and reflections on the possible future of Australia in the final part.

That was the blueprint. The building might be very different. Much of the creative work was done in post-production at our Bristol studio, where as producer I consulted Mike Walker and Andrew Lawrence, the chief BBC technician over the final mix.

We have spent a long time on this particular programme, but I should like to take you through a few more edited highlights, to demonstrate a few more possible elements and ways of assembling them. With cheaper and more efficient digital editing software, we are entering the age of a one person director/author/editor and this may be the way you, the reader/writer/director, may like to work in the future.

A little later in the programme:

INTRODUCE QUIET, SLIGHTLY OMINOUS MUSIC

MAN: We were all brainwashed. The Messiah had offered us the world, but three years down the track we realised he was just a politician.

MANNING-   He was a charismatic personality, but he was in CLARKE: the great river of life . . .

THE MUSIC COMPLEMENTS THE THEME.

                 . . . Things went wrong – Partly because Gough was not a very good judge of other men and he made some tragic mistakes in the choice of people to work with.

WOMAN: His fatal flaw was to try to do too much too soon.

MAN: The fear of change began to seep darkly into the bottoms of the bellies of all of us.

NARRATOR: Nature, so often a force in Australian life, chose to exhibit its power in 1974 when the city of Darwin was struck by Cyclone Tracey.

LOSE MUSIC. THREE SECONDS' SILENCE (THE CALM BEFORE THE STORM)

WOMAN 2:   We had two small earth tremors and the mangoes ripened very early and all the ants were in frenetic activity. Well, the Aborigines know their signs and in the two weeks before Cyclone Tracey some of the old Aborigines just rolled up their swags and left.

ACTUALITY NEWS BROADCAST (HISSY QUALITY)

NEWSCASTER: And here's the latest cyclone warning. At three Cyclone Tracey was centred 80 kilometres north west of Darwin and moving south easterly at seven kilometres per hour.

MIX OF THOUSANDS OF FROGS CROAKING WITH RADIOPHONIC MUSIC

WOMAN 2:   And then the frogs started. And Illiwara the old Aborigine said, 'If the frogs sing out very loud, well then look out'. They started off in a slow chorus and then by the time dusk fell it was a screaming frenzy.

HEIGHTEN MUSIC AND FROG EFFECTS

WOMAN 3:   (shouting above the din) We came home about six o'clock. We had to fill everything we had with water, lock the windows, seal the doors.

LOSE FROGS AND MUSIC. INTRODUCE SLIGHT WIND

WOMAN 2:   You heard a distant moaning and then it got louder and louder. I was going to put my daughter in the Landrover and make a run for it, but my husband said just look out there and clumps of trees were rushing past the house and some people did try to make a run for it and were killed.

STEEPLY INCREASE NOISE OF BUFFETING WIND

WOMAN 4:   Ours was a tropical house with louvres. The wind could get out. In houses where it couldn't get out, they just exploded with the pressure.

WOMAN 5:   There was a great tree at the back of our house and in that tree there was a refrigerator.

INTERVIEWER: You were under the bed with your Mummy?

SMALL GIRL: Yeah, it was terrible.

MIX WIND INTO 'AFTERMATH' MUSIC

WOMAN 2:   When the daylight came we looked out on a scene of utter desolation. Where trees and houses had been there were just stumps and rubble.

MAN: I saw a boat half way up a hill.

After a few more speeches describing the aftermath:

LOSE MUSIC

EMERGENCY BROADCAST (FROM THE TIME):

People of Darwin, this is General Alan Stretton, the civilian chief of the natural disasters organisation.

WOMAN 4:

The looting was indescribable. To me it was like something out of a movie. My daughter was bending over looking at this wedding photograph and, well, a man made an obvious movement . . . I won't go into that, it's too awful and I saw that they were rapists, so I raced and got the gun and I said, 'I'll kill you' and they knew I meant it and they took off.

EMERGENCY BROADCAST:

We must stop rumours. There are rumours about the police shooting people, when in fact it was Tiger Brennan probably shooting the dogs.

WOMAN 3:

And nature reasserted itself. (Giggles) There were people making love all over the place. I passed a house of which there was nothing left except the floorboards and one double bed. It was like Salvador Dali. And there were two people in bed making love, quite oblivious to who might be going past and it didn't matter. (LAUGHS)

BIRDSONG AND CRICKETS AS AT BEGINNING OF PROGRAMME. HOLD FOR SEVERAL SECONDS.

READER:

After the tree falls, there will reign the same silence as stuns and spurs us, enraptures and defeats us, as seems to some a challenge and seems to others to be waiting here for something beyond imagining.

Thus we told the story of Cyclone Tracey, through carefully selected and edited vox pop interviews and through radio broadcasts from the time. We orchestrated or counterpointed the atmosphere with sound effects and with radiophonic music.

I should like to share one final element that we used in this episode: a swearing-in ceremony, in which new Australian citizens are taking the oath of allegiance. Recording it was a moving experience.

ACOUSTIC OF LARGE HALL. QUIET BACKGROUND CHAT AND SINGING, PARTICULARLY OF SMALL CHILDREN, IN MANY LANGUAGES

SWEARING-IN OFFICER:	In a few minutes you will be all equal Australian citizens. At the ceremony we have people here from Yugoslavia, Libya, South Africa, Afghanistan, New Zealand, Turkey, United Kingdom, Vietnam, Chile, Hong Kong, France, Argentina, Portugal, Ireland, Canada, Finland, Pakistan, Indonesia, Philippines, Korea, Malaysia, Spain, Sri Lanka, Greece, Lebanon and Taiwan. (FOLDS PAPER) And that spells multi-culturalism to me. I'm sure it does to you too.

ILLUSTRATING A FIRST PERSON FEATURE

I should like to share with you a more personal feature that I made in the 1980s. It is the kind of feature that you as writer, sound recordist, producer and editor could put together yourself.

I had attended a lecture by a university tutor who, with his 15 year-old son, had cycled through France and Spain along the ancient pilgrimage route to Santiago de Compostella in Galicia. I had saved up some leave and was inspired to do the same with my then 12 year-old son, Seamus. We planned to cut costs, in the five weeks it would take to cycle the 1,100 miles, by taking a tent. At that time, I had in Robin Hicks the most enlightened BBC boss. He was a true enabler and encourager. He said, 'Don't take a tent, that would be like carrying England on your back'. Instead he urged me to take a tape recorder and offered to cover the modest expenses of two poor pilgrims. Furthermore he funded the buying of one of our two new bikes. At the time he was criticised by other BBC managers for profligacy; but the programme came out well under budget and was so popular that it was broadcast four times.

The shape of the programme was simple. It was that of pilgrims, throughout the ages, making the pilgrimage. Seamus and I were simply the most recent among the multitudes who had gone that way before.

Here are the first five minutes. May I suggest you count the elements, scripted speech, actuality, pre-recorded music, etc, and think about how you would plan the shape, and record and assemble these elements. I will explain at the end of the passage.

ANNOUNCER: A reflective pilgrim on the road to Santiago always makes a double journey: The backward journey through time and the forward journey through space.
(INTRODUCE MEDIÆVAL HARP MUSIC BY MARY REMNANT)
Every step the pilgrim makes evokes memories of those who passed that way ever since the discovery of the tomb of the Apostle James in the Ninth Century.

READER: (FROM *JACQUES DE VORAGINES*) When St James was beheaded, his disciples placed his body in a boat without a rudder and an angel of the Lord guided them to Galicia, the Kingdom of Queen Lupa.
When the disciples asked her for a burial place she set them a series of trials. In the last of these they were attacked by two wild bulls. They made the sign of the cross over them and the bulls became as gentle as lambs.
The disciples followed a star, until it stopped. There they buried St James. This was in a field called the field of the star, or Compostella.

ANNOUNCER: 'The Field of the Star.' Last year Shaun MacLoughlin was among the five or six hundred pilgrims who walked or cycled to Santiago de Compostella in Spain. His companion was his son, Seamus.

(FADE MUSIC)

SEAMUS: My dad told me we were going to cycle to Santiago. He just told me, but now I'm glad I went. It was about 1,100 miles and took us around five and a half weeks. I was twelve then, but now I'm thirteen and we both kept diaries.

(<u>ACTUALITY RECORDING OF DEPARTURE</u>)

MOTHER: Just be careful. Right?

SEAMUS: (TO SMALL SISTER) Binnie get off my – Don't put your foot in the pedal, Binnie. The whole thing will tip over.

MOTHER: Right? Right? And just be careful.

SEAMUS: Yeah.

MOTHER: Won't you?

(<u>LOSE ACTUALITY</u>)

SEAMUS: At 3.29 pm we set off for Temple Meads, and I recorded everyone saying good bye.

SHAUN: (<u>A prayer</u>) Please, St James, guide our wheels and bring us safely to your shrine and to heaven.

SEAMUS: And at 4.10 the train set off. At 6.46 the train arrived at Portsmouth Harbour Station. We cycled one and a half miles to the ferry terminal at about seven o'clock. I'm very excited about having to cycle onto the boat.

(<u>INTERWEAVE SOUND EFFECTS OF SEAGULLS AND SEA WASH</u>)

ACTORS AS   (<u>Calling</u>) Pray for us at Santiago, may St James
MEDIÆVAL   look after you, etc.
FRIENDS OF
PILGRIMS:

SEAMUS: The boat rocked all night, up, down, up, down, and it was awful, but I still liked it.

(SAILING BOAT MAKING GOOD WAY. MEDIÆVAL MUSIC)

ACTOR: Haul up the bowline, now, veer the sheet!
Cooke make ready our meat,
Our pilgrims have no lust to eat.
Steward a pot of beer!
Anon of the best.

(MIX FROM MEDIÆVAL MUSIC TO BACKGROUND OF CONTEMPORARY TOURIST CROWD)

SHAUN: After docking at St Malo, we started our pilgrimage proper from Mont St Michel, Normandy, where many pilgrims set out in the Middle Ages.

(ACTUALITY OF GUIDE IN FRENCH)

GUIDE: Ça commence ici la visite à Mont St Michel, etc.

(FADE AS WE MOVE AWAY)

SEAMUS: Mont St Michel was crowded with tourists and very noisy. We left our bicycles by the Gendarmerie –

SHAUN: And walked up the crowded, tripper streets with our heavy packs to the Abbey.

(LOSE CROWDS. BRING UP A MIXED COMMUNITY OF MONKS AND NUNS SINGING PLAINCHANT IN FRENCH)

SHAUN: There we were met by Sister Brigitte and attended Vespers. We had a simple Friday supper and walked round the island with the tide coming up and we had a good night's sleep.
(LOSE PLAINCHANT)
Matins at seven o'clock in the small oratory,

followed by breakfast and Lauds; and then one of the brothers blessed our undertaking.

BROTHER: Benissez espécialment nos deux amis qui maintainant vont partir vers St Jacques de Compostelle, (INTRODUCE GENTLE MEDIÆVAL CHIMES) que l'Apôtre et notre coeur les accompagne sur la route et les ramene sains et saufs dans leur foyer, par Jesus Christ, Notre Seigneur, Amen.

SHAUN: Amen.

SEAMUS: Amen.

This feature was over a year in the making. As you can imagine, cycling up to 50 miles a day with a 12 year-old and finding the route and accommodation was a fulltime activity. We managed to keep diaries, however, most of which we recorded on a family holiday in France the next summer, just before Seamus' voice broke. A generous and talented colleague, John Theocharis, produced it and provided an objective ear. He was able to tell me where I was self-indulgent and should be cut and where Seamus and I were instructive and entertaining and should be retained. John Tydeman described the feature as 'Pilgrim and Adrian Mole'.

9

From Script to Production

PUTTING YOURSELF IN THE PRODUCER'S PLACE

Sometimes the roles of writer and producer may be combined. The playwright Anthony Minghella co-directed his *Cigarettes And Chocolates* with radio drama producer, Robert Cooper. The result was one of the most moving and magical productions I have ever heard.

I believe, however, that this arrangement was an example of the exception that proves the rule. Normally a successful production will be the result of a team effort in which the roles of writer and producer are complementary. Just as a good producer should understand the script as thoroughly as possible, so it can help you, the writer, to take an imaginative leap and to put yourself in the position of the producer. Identifying the producer's problems, disciplines and aspirations should help you to improve your script, which in the final analysis is the blueprint for the production.

In radio the roles of producer, who has overall control of the programme – management, administration and budgeting – and of the director, who has artistic control – involving such decisions as casting, choice of music and interpretation – are combined.

FINDING THE SCRIPT OR IDEA

One can do much to ruin a good script, but one cannot, even with magnificent performances, beautiful music and sensitive pacing and mixing, make a magnificent play out of an uninspired and derivative script.

Thus the producer's first priority must be to find an outstanding script. Unfortunately a producer's time is finite and he will not be able to devote a great deal of attention to every script submitted. In the BBC Script Unit in the 1970s, six of us considered about 200 unsolicited scripts a week. We had a rule that all scripts specifically written for radio, that were neither incoherent nor obscene, should receive a short synopsis and comment. However, to take time on those that were comparatively uninspired was to lose precious time devoted to the more promising. We had to make hard decisions. At today's cost-conscious BBC script readers are more ruthless than we were.

Independent producers' way of working is not so different from that of the BBC in-house producers. Attending writers' seminars, keeping in touch with the writers one knows, coming across talented new writers, through word of mouth and recommendation, and seeing stage plays that would adapt well to radio are all ways of finding new material. One may feel that some plays are not right for radio, but that the writers show promise and that one should meet them to discuss further ideas. At the moment I am working on a theatre production in Vietnam and have come across one or two plays that would translate well to British radio.

However, I prefer to have ideas and scripts that are thought of in the first place in terms of radio. My chief hate is rejected television plays that a writer thinks 'might' make a radio play. The two media could not be more different and it can take more time and creative energy to adapt a television play into a radio play than to write a new radio play from scratch.

We will examine the tricky problem of how to sell your script to the BBC or other outlets in the next chapter.

SCRIPT EDITING, TIMING, ADVERTISING, PRONUNCIATION AND STRONG LANGUAGE

As producer, having found your proposal or your script, you should do everything in your power to help the writer to improve it. However, your guiding principle should be to remain true to the author's intentions. Script-editing, then casting, I regard as the two most vital parts of a producer's job. If you get these right you can almost sit back and enjoy the rest of the production.

Timing
Timing the script is important at this stage. If it is over-long or, more disastrously, under-running for the scheduled slot, then valuable time in the studio and in post-production will be wasted. You will end up with a worse production than you need have done. It is easy to get it wrong. Every writer's dialogue seems, intrinsically, to play at a different pace. How many words there are in a script is irrelevant.

Advertising and pronunciation

Two routine matters to consider are those of advertising and pronunciation. The BBC by its charter is not permitted to promote commercial products. Thus strictly speaking product names such as Hoover, Mercedes or Johnny Walker should not be used. If the writer can find an alternative, time may be saved in the studio. The BBC has a pronunciation unit, though I believe in our accountancy-mad age it now charges internally for this service. So again the more the writer can help the producer to research the correct pronunciation of foreign words, place names, technical terms, etc, the more time and money will be saved at production stage.

Strong language

Strong language is a subject discussed *ad nauseam* within the BBC. The point is often made that in broadcasting a play you are inviting yourself into the privacy of people's homes and that it is courteous therefore to eschew offensive, ugly or scatological language. On the other hand should one apologise for something that one feels is artistically essential?

I should add that in this respect, as in most others, radio works very differently from the visual media. To put it bluntly, if you use the word 'fucking' on radio, that, generally speaking, is the activity that you are inviting the listener to visualise. In all other media the language will be counterpointed – or complemented – by what is happening in sight. Thus for good or ill, strong language can be a much more powerful weapon on radio than in other media.

CASTING

A writer may start with a particular actor in mind for the leading role. As long as he is prepared to leave the question of casting open as the character and the script develop and as the producer becomes involved, this is not a bad idea. It can sometimes lend an extra dimension and it can serve as shorthand between writer and producer.

Time is always at a premium in the studio. Compared with other media, one has virtually no time for rehearsal, so the actor who is 'right' for the part and who comes to the studio prepared is absolutely vital. If as producer I realise that an actor has not done sufficient homework, I tend to forget him when it comes to future casting. Fortunately there are too many dedicated and talented actors competing for work to leave room for those who are careless or lazy.

I admit that, because studio time is at such a premium, I tend to cast 'safely' and to use those actors whom I already know well. One's first responsibility is to the listener, then to the writer and only then to the actors.

I find I generally cast well when I 'listen' to the play at my first reading. I tend to hear the voices. In fact it is almost as if some-one else does the casting. I sometimes confuse actors by saying: 'You'd better ask the other Shaun MacLoughlin for a part'. If my first choice of actor is not available, then I start to agonise. It is crucial to get the casting right.

BUDGETING

Many costs are fixed. There is little room for manoeuvre over the price of the studio, the editing channels, the technicians' hourly rates, the copyright payment. The last is by agreement between the broadcasting organisations and the Society of Authors and The Writers' Guild. Thus the variables, upon which pressure is invariably exerted, are the size of the cast and the length of time required for recording and post-production. There is a growing tendency not to use drama studios, which are expensive to rent, especially in London, but to record on location.

The cost of post-production comes down fairly radically if one invests in the appropriate computer software and learns to operate it oneself. However, this can be time consuming, while artistically one may lose the objectivity provided by another pair of ears.

I normally persuade writers to keep the play technically as simple as possible; but I am wary of allowing budgetary pressures to inhibit artistic pioneering and an innovative and experimental use of the medium.

At my second reading I work out a pattern of scheduling scenes or sequences, so that I can record out of order to save on actors' days. It is particularly important when, for example, I am bringing actors from London to Bristol, to save on expenses. I also work out possible doubling. On the following page is such an example of a scheduling table. I enjoyed the fantasy casting.

DREAM – Casting schedule. Read-through Mon 4, Record Tue 5 to Sat 9 Nov									
Act/Scene	1.1	1.2	5.1	4.1	4.2	3.1	3.2	2.1	2.2
Length (in lines)	250	103	428	216	40	196	463	286	162
DAY	TUE		WED	THUR			FRI	SAT	
Theseus	Patrick Stewart	TH		TH	TH					
Egeus	Bill Wallis	EG			EG					
Lysander	Robert Glenister	LY		LY	LY			LY		LY
Demetrius	Iain Glen	DE		DE	DE			DE	DE	DE
Philostrate/Snug/Lion	Timothy West		SNU	PH/SN			SNU			
Quince/Prologue	Bob Hoskins		QU	QU		QU	QU			
Bottom/Pyramus	Anthony Hopkins		BT	BT	BT	BT	BT			BT
Flute/Thisbe	Tony Robinson		FL	FL		FL	FL			
Snout/Wall	Christian Rodska		SNO	SNO			SNO			
Starveling/Moon	Cornelius Garrett		ST	ST		ST	ST			
Hippolyta/Peasebloss	Diana Rigg	HP		HP	H/P	PE	PE		PE	PE
Hermia/Cobweb	Carolyn Backhouse	HR			H/C	H/C	CO	HR		H/C
Helena/Mustardseed	Jenny Funnell	HL			H/M	H/M	MU	HL		H/M
Oberon	Daniel Day Lewis			OB	OB	OB		OB	OB	OB
Titania/Moth	Juliet Stevenson			TI	TI	T/M	T/M		TI	T/M
Puck	Jean-Marc Perret		PU	PU	PU	PU	PU	PU	PU	PU

This exercise is almost entirely to save on the budget. Patrick Stewart and Bill Wallis will not be required on Thursday or Friday and all the 'mechanicals', except Bottom, will not be required on the Saturday. Supposing Christian Rodska, playing Snout, is offered a day's filming or voiceover work on the Thursday, then he can be released. The only time we should have the entire cast together would be for the read-through.

ORGANISING PUBLICITY AND PROMOTION

In the rush and business of production, this is often an important job that gets overlooked. This is a great pity – if radio drama had enjoyed a higher profile over the past 20 years, it might not have got stuck in Bintian doldrums.

Within the BBC, part of one's routine as a producer is to compile a Promotion Note, with information about star casting and anything else that is newsworthy. This goes to the Channel Controller, who decides whether the programme should be given promotion and publicity priority as the lead of the day or of the week. The best publicity will always emanate from the personal enthusiasm of those actually working on the programme, who will understand its intentions, have first hand knowledge and commitment and may well see an unusual and eye-catching publicity angle. Since I have left the BBC I have found that a few phone calls to journalist friends, accompanied with an invitation to sit in on the studio production, have more than paid dividends. If you are promoting and selling plays on the Internet, the design and 'information architecture' of Web pages is particularly important.

INCORPORATING MUSIC

We have covered the use of commercial recordings earlier. Some composers will write for live musicians. Others will create electronic music in their own studio. In either case the producer should receive a rough draft of the music before going into the studio, so that he can then gauge, during the recording, how the music will match the performances. Usually the music will be dubbed on afterwards, leaving the producer and editor to fine tune the right levels.

USING SOUND EFFECTS

The BBC has a vast library of pre-recorded sound effects, while many independent studios are building up similar collections. Students on media courses often go out with DAT recorders and create their own sound effects. It is important that, whatever facilities one does or does not have, one prepares this as much as possible before recording in the studio.

Some years ago I produced *God's Revolution* by Don Taylor, an original twelve-episode Classic Serial about Cromwell and the Levellers. It contained numerous battle scenes, mostly on horseback. A technician and I recorded horse-riding effects in and around a stables deep in the countryside. We had to achieve single horses and groups of horses, starting from standing still and then galloping, trotting and walking away on soft and on hard surfaces. We had to record travelling with the horse – or horses. We had to record the horses arriving and stopping, both from the point of view of a rider and from the point of view of the person being approached. It was a long day's work, but a healthy and enjoyable one.

Champagne and its possible after-effects

The other kind of spot effects are live or 'practical' that one creates physically in the studio. My favourite sequence is opening a bottle of champagne and pouring out a glass and then, perhaps a little later, being sick.

If the budget does not run to several bottles of bubbly (for re-takes), one uses a sawn off bicycle pump with a cork stuffed into it, that one then pumps and pops out. Then one pours water into a glass, close to the mike, adding Alka Seltzer or Beechams Powder to create the necessary fizz. To create the effect of being sick, one needs a hot water bottle filled with water, but without the stopper. The actor clasps it to his chest and then leans forward, retching as he goes, until with perfect timing and action the contents slurp onto the floor.

It can be a good idea, particularly on a complex production, to have a planning meeting with the technicians to discuss the overall approach and in particular any special sound effects required. You need to be aware that some technicians, particularly those comparatively new to radio drama, may be over literal about sound effects. They may not realise that the actual noise of say a car swerving will not create the required image in the listener's mind. This needs very careful thought. A technician may say to me, 'But this is a recording of a Rolls Royce,' when all one hears is a gentle hum that could evoke almost anything. Sometimes one needs to explain that simply because the play stipulates a busy London Street, one does not need to hear a continuous heavy noise of traffic. In real life, subjectively, we often block out such noises from our consciousness.

At the planning meeting one can also discuss the overall schedule in the studio and any unusual approaches one wishes to take. If one intends to record all or any of the play on location, careful and thorough planning is needed to find the right locations, organise transport to and fro, and have fall back, contingency plans in case of violent, ie noise-making rain or continuous interruptions by unwanted other noises. (Incidentally a pretty and charming actress to persuade a farm labourer to leave his tractor and go for a pint of cider can be a real asset.)

PREPARING THE ACTORS

If there is a particular problem for an actor, such as difficult pronunciations, an unusual accent or something ambiguous in the script, then a letter or phone call may save considerable time in the studio. You may wish to give them some background information that is not contained in the script. With these problems the playwright should be able to help. In any case, it is vital to get the script to the actors as early as you can, so that they have ample preparation time.

Some star actors will require a degree of cosseting. They may like a car to collect them and if they are staying in a hotel, make sure they are well looked after and feel loved. Such care on the part of the producer and production assistant can pay real dividends. It is vital to create a happy working atmosphere in the studio.

GETTING INTO THE STUDIO

At last the preparation is over and the most enjoyable part of the production can begin. The studio is divided into the control room, from where the main part of the production team will record and monitor the play; and the studio proper, a series of soundproof acoustic spaces where the actors and floor manager will operate.

There will also be a 'green room' for the actors to relax in between takes.

For many years I was fortunate to work at Christchurch Drama Studio, Bristol. This is a magical and inspiring building that in its time has been a brewery warehouse, a village school and a couple of Church of England halls. The entire building is wired for microphones, talk-back and cue lights. I once, illegally, used the air conditioning unit to record the action and sound effects for a shoot out in a container ship. It had the right acoustic. There is a fully practical kitchen where, with the window open to the resonant courtyard at the side of the studio, I have recorded scenes in a fishmongers. The cellars with their connecting stairs and corridors are marvellous for Shakespearean dungeons and Nazi torture chambers. Best of all is the 'dead room' or anachoic chamber, where outdoor scenes are recorded. (It is called 'dead', because the acoustic is not 'live' or echoey, but absorbent.) There is an 'acoustic trap', a padded bending corridor, leading off the dead room, in which one can create war cries and cavalry charges approaching from half a mile away. This studio is an inspiration to all who work there and greatly loved throughout the profession.

The production team consists of the producer, the production assistant (who keeps a record of the timing of each scene or sequence, of how many 'takes' there may be and of any 'fluffs' and 'go-backs'), the senior studio manager, who operates the mixing desk, controls the balance and is responsible to the producer for all technical matters, including playing in any music and recorded sound effects and for monitoring that the play is actually recorded. If time permits, the grams operator may also assemble the chosen takes and begin on the post-production – perhaps as the producer is rehearsing the next scene. The final member of the production team is the floor manager, who works with the actors in the studio. She is responsible to the producer and to the senior studio manager for what happens 'on the floor', for calling the actors from the green room and for creating, or delegating the actors to create, the practical, 'spot' effects.

The writer's role
The writer is usually invited to be present in the control room. It is the mark of a good producer to use the writer as constructively as possible, in fact as part of the production team. After all it is

the writer who has first 'heard' the play and who should have a great deal of value to contribute.

Rehearsing and recording

There are two basic ways to rehearse and record a radio play. The more common is called 'Rehearse/Record'. This means breaking the play down into convenient, recordable sequences, preferably, but not necessarily, in the order of the play and then rehearsing and recording each sequence in turn.

The other way is to rehearse the entire play first and then to record it in one go, or at least in as long sequences as are technically feasible to accomplish. Different producers and actors prefer different methods. I tend to use the first method, because I work mostly in Bristol and, in say a three day production, my budget may only stretch to some London based actors for one or two days. I may therefore have to record the scenes affecting those actors out of sequence. Many actors prefer this method as it means total concentration for shorter, intenser periods. They can relax between takes. Others favour recording the play in a single go. They feel that by taking a sweep at it, it can sometimes take off in a way that achieves unexpected depths and greater emotional intensity.

The read-through

In either case I am a passionate believer in the importance of the read-through. This is when the actors with the producer, the writer and the production assistant sit down and read the play together for the first time. The technicians may be present, though they may need to set up the studio and 'build the sets' during this period.

The read-through may be the only opportunity before the final edit to hear the play in its entirety. It is a crucial occasion for the actors to 'offer' their interpretation, for the production assistant to time the play, and for the writer and the producer to respond.

Over the years as a producer, I have tended to say less and less before the read-through. Some of my colleagues give the most brilliant, erudite and fascinating exposés of the script. However, I feel that, if I say too much, I may inhibit an actor from offering an interesting and valuable interpretation that neither the writer nor I have foreseen.

After the read-through, with reference to the writer, I hope to give the most crucial notes. It may often be a case of two leading actors offering a very different interpretation, so that they hardly appear to be in the same play. A compromise has to be sought. There may be some background information, an anecdote about a person or place or the writer's motive for writing the play, that the actors will find enlightening. The appropriateness of accents, particularly where an actor has to double or treble parts, may need to be examined. The few minutes after the read-through can be a very fertile period.

A paradoxical problem occurs when an actor gives what one considers to be a perfect reading. Actors like something to chew upon. They like to feel they are progressing, that they have somewhere to go; so it is not actually very helpful to tell them that what they have done is perfect and to ask them simply to repeat themselves. I therefore always try to say something to them, even if it is upon a minor point of information or a quibble about the pronunciation of a single word.

Generally criticism must be constructive. There simply is not time in the studio to break an actor's confidence and then to build it up again. I remember the story of a dear colleague, who miscast a part disastrously. During a rehearsal when he was producing from the control room, he put his head in hands in despair, murmured, 'Oh my God!', took a deep breath, went out into the studio and lied enthusiastically: 'That was absolutely wonderful, darling! Now let's build on it: point 1 . . . point 2 . . . point 3 . . . point 4 . . .'

I like, if possible, to have the first lunch break after the read-through to give the actors – and myself and the writer – time to mull over what has passed and what we want to achieve. Ideally I like to have the read-through the day before recording. That is not always possible, simply for budgetary reasons; but artistically to allow a night to sleep on the read-through can be invaluable.

Reading the nitty-gritty
Once the Rehearse/Record proper begins, some producers tend to rehearse in the studio, where they can relate more directly to the actors. Others stay more in the control room, where they can relate more directly to the listener – and to the writer and the technicians. I tend to play it by ear and vary my approach, but I think that as producer my primary function is to identify with the listener. (I often keep my eyes closed.) In fact I have to attempt to be a sort of 'archetypal' listener. I may even invite a sympathetic visitor to the studio to share this function.

Reacting to the rehearsal

If I listen from the control room, at the end of a scene's rehearsal, I press the talk back button, thank the actors and tell them I shall shortly be with them. I then digest as quickly as possible the writer's and the senior studio manager's reactions. Generally I do not invite the writer to speak directly to the actors as this can consume too much precious time. Also the writer may not be practised in how to get the best out of the actors. Armed with my own thoughts and those of my colleagues, I then, hastily, think how to translate these into constructive notes and so I enter the studio.

Knowing what not to say is as important as knowing what to say. I try to keep my notes to a minimum. I like to leave 'spaces' for the actors to fill in, to make their own.

After I have given the actors their notes, I generally go for the first take. Although this may be a little early, it will tend to concentrate minds and energies. I often find at this stage, that in their performance I can hear the actors thinking about the notes I have given them. They are on the right lines, but sound a little stilted. I therefore thank them very nicely and ask them to have another go, making the notes their own. This second take I usually find elicits the best performance that one is liable to get within the limited time at one's disposal. Often at this point the actors discover spontaneity and energy; they catch the character, as it were, upon the wing. If one had days to rehearse, as in most other media, one might come back to and surpass this point. However, I usually find that, if one flogs a scene too much, staleness sets in.

If I have time, I go back towards the end of the recording period to the opening of the play and re-record it. By then the actors should be more deeply into their characters and be able to offer something more compelling.

Different producers will have very different approaches and the more producers that you as a writer can work with the better. You may grow to totally disagree with what I have just said and, if you do, I am sure it will be very healthy.

DOING LOCATION DRAMA

Particularly in London with the rising cost of studios, there is a growing tendency to record on location. A 'dry' studio, that is one without technicians, can cost at least £1,000 a day; whereas on location one has only the cost of a portable recorder – and possibly added transport and catering costs.

This is generally only appropriate in contemporary plays, because there are few locations completely free of the sound of distant traffic, farm machinery or the flight path of aeroplanes. Even with a play in a modern setting one may be subject to time-consuming interruptions that will add to the pressure and the budget. (I do know of one or two deep valleys, near Bristol, that are almost always quiet.)

When things are working well as they did for me when I recorded *Whee 'Oss* by R E T Lamb, a play set in Padstow in Cornwall on Mayday, the result can be magical. The actors found themselves inspired by the setting and we were able to achieve a sense of space that in the studio, even with Christchurch Studio's acoustic trap, would have been impossible. We recorded one scene at night in a garden about half a mile from the distant celebrations in the fishing town. There was a sense of holiness in the air and the actors instinctively lowered their voices. I don't think I would have thought to have given them that direction in the studio.

The first play that I recorded entirely on location was by the poet and travel writer, Paul Hyland. It was called *Dancing Ledge*, named after an artificial cave quarried out of the rock on the Purbeck peninsula in Dorset. We had actors running in and out of the cave, calling to each other on a ledge just above the sea. This was something else that could not have been achieved in the studio.

My personal best location moment was in Australia. I recorded in the National Park, south of Sydney, a scene about the White Australian gold diggers beating up Chinese coolies. It was an improvised scene and one inspired Australian actor went tearing off into the bush, pursuing an imaginary coolie and yelling, in a very politically incorrect manner, 'Ching-Chong-Chinaman'. At this precise moment a kookaburra chose to let off its mocking, unearthly laugh. It was the end of the scene and I was worried that my friend Andrew, the BBC technician, had faded out too early, but he gave me the thumbs up.

Peter Terson wrote a series of what he called 'landscape plays', in which we developed a technique of mixing studio and location. For example, scenes in the chief character's memory or in his fantasy might take place in the abstract, controlled setting of the studio with only remembered or imagined sound effects, while scenes in the present storyline might take place on location with the more intrusive and accidental sounds of the everyday world. This technique gave a nice variety and contrast to the texture of the play.

EDITING

I generally find that recording is a euphoric time and post-production or editing is a deeply depressing experience. It is then, as producer, that one hears all the mistakes one has made; all the notes one has *not* given to the actors and technicians.

However, I have to come to realise that this also is the time to use one's depression professionally, to rectify mistakes as much as possible. It is remarkable what can be achieved with state of the art, digital, editing software and the speed with which it can be done. You can change the actors' timing and their level or 'presence'. You can dub on music and sound effects. You can even, up to a point, play with the pitch, 'the top' or 'bottom' or modify the stereo 'picture' to lessen the effects of over obtrusive or unwanted sound effects. However, this all takes valuable and expensive time and it is, of course, better not to have made such mistakes in the first place.

10

Marketing Your Script, and the Future

WRITING FOR THE BBC

For 75 years the BBC was the guardian of the great British tradition of radio drama. During the recent Birt era fashionable jargon such as 'centres of excellence', 'producer choice' and 'accountability' in practice meant the precise opposite of what they claimed. It was not surprising that this double-speak damaged radio drama and staff morale and drove writers away from the medium. Liz Forgan, ex-Managing Director of BBC Radio put it more diplomatically: 'Real radio – programmes made by people whose passion and brillance is in making pictures with sound – are not necessarily great audience-getters.'

However I am pleased to report that the quality and quantity of BBC radio drama and also staff morale are showing signs of recovery. When I made enquiries for this edition my ex-colleagues were positive and helpful. Helen Boaden, Controller Radio 4 wrote:

> We do a huge amount of drama and, inevitably, some of it falls short of what we had hoped for . . . I want radio drama to continue to flourish . . . One of our great challenges is to woo new listeners – many of whom have not grown up with speech radio as their first medium – into the pleasures of radio drama. Our drama output has to chime with the intelligence and curiosity of our listeners and should offer a diversity of style, format and content which I know our audience expects. It is incredibly important that writers for Radio 4 listen across the network and understand the very broad range of interests and tastes that we serve . . . It is important that we maintain a balance between new writing and established writers who have an instinctive feel for Radio 4.

Kate Rowland, Head of the New Writing Initiative, added:

Radio drama has a real commitment to new writers, with schemes operating to find talent from the Alfred Bradley Bursary Award in the North, Chasing the Rainbow in the Midlands and Sparks across the whole country. The Wire on R3 represents the best of new contemporary writing – the network is constantly looking to reflect drama as it happens – writers at the forefront – bold, popular storytellers. We are committed to represent a diversity of voices and this year 10 per cent of radio drama's output will be from black and Asian writers. Radio drama can touch the audience in a very direct way and provoke a large audience response, for example *Spoonface Steinberg*, *Postcards from Shannon*, *The Lockerbie Letters* and Benjamin Zephaniah's drama *Listen To Your Parents*. The BBC is unique in its ability to deliver to the audience the epic, the familiar and the extraordinary, e.g. *Nicholas Nickleby* returning to Dickens' original serial form, *2000 Tales* reflecting Chaucer in urban Britain – 21 writers, 50 actors on two networks – and in the New Year an oral dramatisation of the *Bayeux Tapestry* on R4 and the Web, which takes us into the living heart of the tapestry, written by Simon Armitage and Jeff Young, with up-to-the minute news reports from *Kirsty Wark*.

Choosing your programme slot

The following are subject to change, but provide an idea of what the BBC is looking for. On Radio 4 the Commissioning Editor's comments are as follows:

Woman's Hour Drama, 15' daily serial: Dramatisations and new work, not a slot for beginners. *Afternoon Play, 45'*. Single plays with occasional series. Huge range of material from new work to dramatisations, drama documentaries, mysteries, thrillers, crime and biographical pieces. *Friday Play, 60'*. Single works that test the medium of radio. Unlikely to be place for beginners unless they have track record in either theatre or film or television already. *Saturday Play, 60'*. Single plays that must have very strong narrative. Crime, romance, mysteries and thrillers encouraged. *Classic Serial, 60'*. Serialisations of extant works of fiction. Not a slot for beginners. Writers interested in this area should check with Commissioning Editor's office at Radio 4 whether the title is already under commission or has been recently broadcast.

There is also comedy on Radio 4: *Monday – Friday 11.30–12.00.* Narrative. Reviving, energising and cheery. *Monday – Thursday 18.30–19.00.* Sitcom, broken comedy or sketch shows, Family entertainment. *Friday 18.30.* Satire. *Tuesday, Wednesday and Thursday 23.00–23.30.* Top comedy performers and writers. New comic ideas and forms. Sharp wit and intelligence rather than surreal. *Children's Drama.* It is rumoured (*Whitaker's Almanac 2001*) that Radio 4 will be reviving some.

On Radio 3 the *Sunday Play* consists of major classics, 'radical plays' and new theatre plays. This is the only regular slot for full-length plays on radio. There is a new experimental writing slot for which Kate Rowland is responsible, as she is for the *Friday Play*.

Looking for full-length plays
Until the late 1980s Radio 4 broadcast two 75- or 90-minute plays a week. Now there are no plays over an hour's length (except on rare occasions). Writers are no longer encouraged to explore the medium with the depth and freedom that has contributed much to the nation's artistic life. Since Radio 5 abandoned its inspired commitment to children's drama and now devotes itself to sport and news, one wonders whether an hourly fix of news on Radio 4 as well is really essential. Many listeners resent being deprived of the radio equivalent of the feature film or full-length stage play except on a Sunday night on Radio 3. They resent being presumed to have a diminishing concentration span. Helen Boaden says: 'I would very much like to produce more [90-minute plays] but this depends on budgets.' One hopes that the Director General will soon fulfil his commitment to putting money into programmes.

Submitting your scripts
Under the present system you must surmount two hurdles. You must be both writer and self-promoter. Perseverance pays dividends. There are several possible approaches:

1. Find a sympathetic producer. To do this listen to as many productions as possible and decide which producers' taste and style seem appropriate to your work. If they like it, they in turn

will have to submit your script to a commissioning editor, but at least you will have a friend and advocate at court.

2. Submit to the New Writing Co-ordinator (in March 2001 this was Jessica Dromgoole) at Broadcasting House, Portland Place, London W1A 1AA. She receives about 200 scripts and ideas for radio and television drama a week. Your script or idea will then be looked at by a team of freelance readers, who once a month sift through submissions and select and take away what look like the most promising 20 per cent or so of submissions for a thorough appraisal and report. The remainder will be returned with a standard rejection letter. In the 1970s when I was a radio drama script editor we used to receive about 300 scripts a week just for radio and we used to report on about 90 per cent of submissions. If the BBC were to devote a larger proportion of licence-payers' money to programmes, more writers could receive constructive feedback. There is no harm in reminding the BBC of its responsibility in this regard.

3. If you live in a national region you can submit to Patrick Rayner in Scotland, Alison Hindell in Wales or Anne Simpson in Northern Ireland. Submissions for the Northern and Midlands English Regions have been subsumed by London.

4. Bristol's documentary feature-making department is interested in drama with a documentary side to it that uses poetry or has a literary aspect. Unless you are offering ideas, which fall into these areas they are not an ideal place to submit your work. Producers are Jeremy Howe, Tim Dee, Viv Beeby, Sara Davies, Paul Dodgson, Mary Ward Lowery and Kate McAll. If you like their work, submit direct to them.

5. There is a targeted scheme run by the New Writing Initiative. They invite you to let them know if there is a reading, production or screening of your work which they will try and see.

6. Finally, 10 per cent of radio drama is by independent producers. See the list at the end of the book for those who consider unsolicited scripts and treatments. Please note that most are based in the south-east or north of England. Try to find a producer who does not live too far from where you do.

I also suggest you contact the New Writing Initiative to ask for the leaflet: *Writing Drama for BBC Radio and Television – Guidelines for Unsolicited Work.*

The above pattern and personnel may change and it is advisable to make enquiries on a regular basis. The BBC claims to belong to and be accountable to the licence-payer. A persistent and courteous stream of letters, enquiring how the nation may continue to have the freedom to speak to itself through its writers should spur the BBC's management to encourage this vital element in our democracy.

WRITING FOR ONEWORD

Since the first edition of this book there has been a promising development in the world of commercial radio. Paul Kent, Head of programmes at Oneword has this to say:

Oneword is the world's first commercial radio station exclusively dedicated to plays, books and comedy. It broadcasts 18 hours a day, seven days a week on digital radio, Sky Digital TV (point 942) and on the Internet at www.oneword.co.uk.

We went on air on May 2nd 2000.

At the moment, Oneword is broadcasting audio books, features and plays that are already commercially available. Because we have only recently started, and we receive no licence fee, we have to earn every penny we spend. This unfortunately means that at present our production budget is minuscule. Digital radio is still in its infancy (but growing fast), and what we believe to be a sizeable audience on Sky and the Internet is not accepted currency when it comes to negotiating advertising rates. In addition we have only six staff. Total. We are decidedly NOT Radio 4, as witnessed by the fact that we run our entire operation on three-quarters of one per cent of their budget!

However, we feel it is important to establish a presence in the media landscape, and, having told you of the reality of our situation, the rest of what I have to say will be resolutely upbeat. So don't stop reading yet!

We have already produced two dramatised readings, which we commissioned ourselves – one concerning Jack the Ripper, the second about a stowaway on board the *Titanic*. I shall go into some detail about both, as they will give some idea of what is feasible at present.

The Whitechapel Murders was based on a guided walk round the East End of London given by Jenny March, an acknowledged expert on the subject, and whose trip I had greatly enjoyed. Jenny came to our studios, and delivered her talk as though she was taking a tour party round the sites of these grizzly crimes. Library sound FX and music were added, and, hey presto! – a one-hour programme was created, which we transmitted on Hallowe'en night.

Constance was written by Rosalind Hutton, an unpublished author currently attending a creative writing course. Her script so impressed me that we decided to produce a version of it. Again, the format was single voice, with music and effects, but nonetheless powerful for that. Rosalind, as an unpublished writer, now has a CD of a broadcast work which she can use in any way she likes to further her career. And the moral of the story is that while Oneword is unable to offer much in the way of remuneration, we can help new writers get started, put extra lines on their CVs, and break the vicious circle which insists that you can't be taken seriously unless you've had something produced.

These are necessarily modest beginnings, and the expansion of our drama output is wholly dependent on appropriate funds being made available. But we'll be aiming high and, eventually, I would like to schedule a soap and a stand-alone piece every day, in addition to the daily Shakespeare series we're planning to launch in April with the help of our friends at Naxos Audio. However, I am not planning to commit to fixed numbers of slots. This is a deliberate policy ensuring that each work will have to earn its place in the schedule.

To sum up what I'm after at this stage: small-scale pieces, no more than an hour in length, casts numbering no more than four, and, please, can we have upbeat themes which don't involve hospitals and illnesses, marital breakdown and child abuse? Drama on Oneword will be about entertaining and challenging our audience, rather than depressing them! It must not be obscure either in subject or treatment, and it most certainly must not be self-indulgent. In addition, there's nothing wrong with raiding those bottom drawers for pieces which may have been rejected elsewhere, but which you feel still deserve an airing.

Oneword is a chance for all of us to have a bit of fun – you won't have to write a ten-page essay every time you submit a piece, and you'll find the commissioning process is short, direct and honest.

And do look at the Website, browse through the schedule, and if you can, have a listen to the tone of the station. Above all, THAT will give you an idea of what we're after. You can contact me on 020 7976 3033 or at paulkent@oneword.co.uk if you'd like a chat about any of the above.

Bear with us . . . Oneword is going to be big news soon.

OTHER MARKETS AND THE FUTURE

Broadcasting, with its set hours of listening, may in the next generation give way to the freedom of choosing what you want to hear, when you want to hear it. I recently talked to a millionaire, who said he believed in vision rather than in audience research. He said, 'Do not talk of radio drama, let's call it sound or audio drama. That is the future'.

In his book *Visions, How Science Will Revolutionise the 21st Century and Beyond*, Michio Kaku outlines an imaginary day in 2020 AD. At breakfast your personal computer will have printed out a personalised edition of the newspaper by scanning the Internet for whatever items are most likely to interest you. In the near future, the cost of computers will plummet and their effectiveness in accessing information and entertainment will multiply. Thus, if we have an interest in audio drama, we may be able to find it, when we want it, out there in the ether – perhaps for a small charge. Tim Crook explores this possibility in his recent book, *Radio Drama*.

As we go to press, some interesting UK sites, where you can listen to streamed audio drama, are www.irdp.co.uk and www.soundplay.co.uk, which also provide information on writing, producing and directing radio drama. Have a look at www.oneword.co.uk (see above) and www.birst.co.uk. Also www.bbc.co.uk/whatson live streams their radio broadcast programme output. If one is not in earshot of the UK radio network then a daily dose of audio drama can be maintained through their Website.

Yuri Rasovsky, www.irasov.com, is probably the most accomplished radio drama producer in the United States. He only gives (very good) samples of his work as he is marketing it commercially. I also recommend www.kcrw.org, the site for

KCRW, the community radio station in Los Angeles, which has been producing weekly drama for over ten years, sometimes in co-production with the BBC. Also sample www.net-entertainment for its science-fiction comedy drama series. It is in five to ten minute episodes, ideal for those who pay by the minute for their phone calls. It has an abundance of interesting and novel sound effects and design. www.profzounds.com contains comedy, drama, sketches and commercials. www.virtuallyamerican.com gathers its content from a variety of theatre companies in the US, including The White Noise Theatre Company, ZBS Foundation and The Natural Broadcast Company. They include RealAudio interviews with some of their contributing producers.

For Australian Internet drama, where you can 'bring out the candles, turn off the lights and close your eyes', go to http://members.tripod.com/~audiodrama/ and find a 'weekly showcase of radio plays from around the world'. If you enjoy French try www.francelink.com and click on 'Radio' and then on 'France Culture' and you can listen to an impressive and varied selection of drama, poetry and radiophonic features.

SIGNING OFF

Writing this book has been a joy. It has been a celebration of an immensely fulfilling vocation. It has also concentrated my mind on the way forward and helped me to found www.soundplay.co.uk with a team of like-minded friends and colleagues. We plan to pioneer 'Audio-led Internet Drama' with creative and highly interactive visuals that can complement and counterpoint the plays, documentaries, readings and poetry that you are listening to, though occasionally we shall invite you to close your eyes to see whether the pictures are better. If you would like to know more please contact me on shaun@soundplay.co.uk.

As I began this book with AMDG I should like to conclude with the postscript that completed my homework at school: LDS (*Laus Deum Semper*) – Praise always to God.

BBC RADIO 4 DRAMA SUPPLIERS WHO ACCEPT UNSOLICITED SCRIPTS (JANUARY 2001)

Company	Contact	Address
Bona Lattie	Turan Ali	9 Beech Houses, Royal Cresent, Margate, Kent CT9 5AL
Catherine Bailey Productions	Catherine Bailey	110 Gloucester Avenue, Primrose Hill, London NW1 8JA
Festival Radio	Antje Strauch	PO Box 107, Brighton BN1 1QG
First Writers	Don Taylor	Lime Kiln Cottage, High Starlings, Banham NR16 2BS
Goldhawk Universal Productions	Jane Quill	20 Great Chapel Street, London W1V 3AQ
Mentorn Radio	Tony Cheevers	43 Whitfield Street, London W1P 6TG
Pier Productions	Peter Hoare	Lower Ground Floor, 1 Marlborough Place, Brighton BN1 1TU
Realize Limited	Michael Fox	Horden Farm, Buston Road, Macclesfield SK11 0AN
Squire Horse Productions	Dave Sheasby	1 Oakhill Road, Netheridge, Sheffield S7 1SJ
The Fiction Factory	John Taylor	Church Street, London SE10 9BJ
Tumble Hill Productions	Jane Dauncey	1 Worleton, Dyffryn, Cardiff CF5 6SW
Watershed Productions	Chris Wallis	16 Church Lane, Marple, Stockport, Cheshire SK6 6DE
Jarvis and Ayres Productions	Martin Jarvis	82 Eaton Terrace, London SW1

Further Reading

The Art of Radio, Donald McWhinnie (Faber & Faber, 1959).
Best Radio Plays of 1978 (and subsequent years to 1991) (Methuen/BBC). **1978**: Richard Harris: *Is it Something I Said?,* Don Haworth: *Episode on a Thursday Evening*, Jill Hyem: *Remember Me*, Tom Mallin: *Halt! Who Goes There?* Jennifer Phillips: *Daughters of Men*, Fay Weldon: *Polaris*. **1979**: Shirley Gee: *Typhoid Mary*, Carey Harrison: *I Never Killed my German*, Barrie Keeffe: *Heaven Scent*, John Kirkmorris: *Coxcomb*, John Peacock: *Attard in Retirement*, Olwyn Wymark: *The Child*. **1980**: Stewart Parker: *The Kamikaze Groundstaff Reunion Dinner*, Martyn Read: *Waving to a Train*, Peter Redgrove: *Martyr of the Hives*, William Trevor: *Beyond the Pale*. **1981**: Peter Barnes: *The Jumping Mimuses of Byzantium*, Don Haworth: *Talk of Love and War*, Harold Pinter: *Family Voices*, David Pownall: *Beef*, J P Rooney: *The Dead Image*, Paul Thain: *The Biggest Sandcastle in the World*. **1982**: Rhys Adrian: *Watching the Plays Together*, John Arden: *The Old Man Sleeps Alone*, Harry Barton: *Hoopoe Day*, Donald Chapman: *Invisible Writing*, Tom Stoppard: *The Dog it was that Died*, William Trevor: *Autumn Sunshine*. **1983**: Wally K Daly: *Time Slip*, Shirley Gee: *Never in my Lifetime*, Gerry Jones: *The Angels They Grow Lonely*, Steve May: *No Exceptions*, Martyn Read: *Scouting for Boys*. **1984**: Stephen Dunstone: *Who is Sylvia?*, Robert Ferguson: *Transfigured Night*, Don Haworth: *Daybreak*, Caryl Phillips: *The Wasted Years*, Christopher Russell: *Swimmer*, Rose Tremain: *Temporary Shelter*. **1985**: Rhys Adrian: *Outpatient*, Barry Collins: *King Canute*, Martin Crimp: *Three Attempted Acts*, David Pownall: *Ploughboy Monday*, James Saunders: *Menocchio*, Michael Wall: *Hiroshima: The Movie*. **1986**: Robert Ferguson: *Dreams, Secrets, Beautiful Lies*, Christina Reid: *The Last of a Dyin' Race*, Andrew Rissik: *A Man Alone: Anthony*, Ken Whitmore: *The Gingerbread House*, Valerie Windsor, *Myths and Legacies*. **1987**: Wally K Daly: *Mary's*,

Frank Dunne: *Dreams of Dublin Bay*, Anna Fox: *Nobby's Day*, Nigel D Moffat: *Lifetime*, Richard Nelson: *Languages Spoken Here*, Peter Tinniswood: *The Village Fete*. **1988**: Ken Blakeson: *Excess Baggage*, Terence Frisby: *Just Remember Two Things: It's Not Fair and Don't Be Late*, Anthony Minghella: *Cigarettes and Chocolate*, Rona Munro: *The Dirt under the Carpet*, Dave Sheasby: *Apple Blossom Afternoons*. **1989**: Elizabeth Baines: *The Baby Buggy*, Jennifer Johnston: *O Ananias, Azarias and Misael*, David Zane Mairowitz: *The Stalin Sonata*, Richard Nelson: *Eating Words*, Craig Warner: *By Where the Old Shed Used to Be*. **1990**: Tony Bagley: *The Machine*, David Cregan: *A Butler Did It*, John Fletcher: *Death and the Tango*, Tina Pepler: *Song of the Forest*, Steve Walker: *The Pope's Brother*. **1991**: Robin Glendinning: *The Words are Strange*, John Purser: *Carver*, Tom Stoppard: *In the Native State*, Steve Walker: *Mickey Mookey*, Craig Warner: *Figure with Meat*.

British Radio Drama, ed. John Drakakis, contains chapters on radio plays of Samuel Beckett, Giles Cooper, Susan Hill, Louis MacNiece, Henry Reed, Dorothy Sayers and Dylan Thomas (Cambridge University Press, 1981).

Collected Shorter Plays of Samuel Beckett includes radio plays: *All That Fall, Embers, Rough for Radio I, Rough for Radio II, Words and Music, Cascando* (Faber, 1989).

Contacts (The Spotlight, London). A useful guide to professional organisations.

Lake Woebegon Days, Garrison Keillor (Faber, 1985).

The Man Born to be King, Dorothy Sayers (Ignatius Press, San Francisco, 1943).

Prospero and Ariel, D G Bridson (Victor Gollancz, 1971).

Radio Acting, Alan Beck (A&C Black, 1997).

Radio Drama, Theory and Practice, Tim Crook (Routledge, 1999).

Radio Drama, Ian Rodger (Macmillan Press, 1982).

Radio Plays: An Epiphanous Use of the Microphone, Beef, Ploughboy Monday, Flos, Kitty Wilkinson, Under the Table, David Pownall (Oberon, 1998).

A Radio Romance, Garrison Keillor (Faber, 1991).

Spoonface Steinberg and Other Plays, Lee Hall (BBC Books, 1997).

Squirrel's Cage and Other Microphone Plays, Tyrone Guthrie (Cobden & Sanderson, 1931).

The Stuff of Radio, Lance Sieveking (Cassell, 1934).

Understanding Media: The Extension of Man, Marshall McLuhan (MIT Press, 1995).

The Way To Write Radio Drama, William Ash (Elm Tree Books, 1985).

Whose is the Kingdom: nine part radio series, John Arden (Methuen, 1988).

Writing for Radio, Colin Haydn Evans (Allison & Busby, 1991).

Writing for Radio, Rosemary Horstmann (A & C Black, 3rd edition, 1997). Contains script of *This Gun in My Right Hand is Loaded*, by Timothy West.

Writing Radio Drama, Keith Richards (Currency Press, Sydney, 1991).

Used in the text

Giles Cooper: Six Plays for Radio (BBC Publications, 1966).

The Hitch-Hiker's Guide to the Galaxy, Douglas Adams. Copyright Serious Productions Ltd, reprinted by permission of Pan Books.

A Suffolk Trilogy, Carey Harrison (Daedelus Press, 1982).

This Gun in My Right Hand is Loaded, Timothy West (A & C Black, 3rd edition, 1997).

The Vernacular Republic, Poems 1961–1981, Les A Murray (Angus & Robertson).

Visions, Michio Kaku (OUP, 1998).

. . . and thanks to

Discovering the Art of Wireless, Tina Pepler (unpublished thesis).

Index

WRITING FOR TELEVISION
How to write and sell successful TV scripts

William Smethurst

'If would-be TV scriptwriters are looking for a wide-ranging
and practical book to light the fuse which could lead to a
successful career, they should certainly invest in a copy.'
BAFTA News.

192 pages. 1 85703 666 2. 3rd edition

THE WRITER'S GUIDE TO RESEARCH
An invaluable guide to gathering material for features, novels
and non-fiction books

Marion Field

Whether you are writing fact or fiction, good research is
essential if you want to add authority and vitality to your work.
This valuable resource book gives thorough help on conducting
effective research, shows how to find the material you need, and
how to use it. Find out how to save time *and* improve the quality
of your information. Marion Field is an experienced freelance
writer and has published both articles and biographies. She
is the author of several reference books for writing including
Improving Your Written English.

104pp. illus. 1 85703 574 7. 2nd edition

AWAKEN THE WRITER WITHIN
How to discover and release your true writer's voice

Cathy Birch

'Takes you on a journey into the subconscious to help you find that voice –and use it. The results can be both amazing and satisfying.' *Writers' Own.* There is a solid, practical base to Cathy's book . . . Give Cathy's methods a try, you might surprise yourself.' *Writers' Bulletin.*

144 pages. 1 85703 656 5. 2nd edition

CREATIVE WRITING
Use your imagination, develop your writing skills and get published

Adèle Ramet

Do you dream of writing short stories or novels, factual articles or non-fiction books? This guide shows you how to improve every area of your writing. 'A book which merits a place on every writer's bookshelf.' *Writers' Bulletin.* Adèle Ramet writes short and twist-in-the-tale stories and non-fiction articles and is a creative writing tutor.

136 pages. 1 85703 699 9. 3rd edition

WRITER'S GUIDE TO COPYRIGHT AND LAW
Get your full financial reward and steer clear of legal pitfalls
Helen Shay

'Vital information for every writer.' *Writer's Book Society.*
'Very informative and useful – I wish our legal editors could manage to put their books into such plain language.'
Barnes & Taylor Solicitors.

96 pages. 1 85703 551 8. 2nd edition

WRITING YOUR LIFE STORY
How to record and present your memories for future generations to enjoy
Michael Oke

This clear step-by-step guide is packed with hundreds of ideas, memory joggers and techniques to bring your personal or family story to life. You can write a comprehensive record or a series of memories and anecdotes. This guide will show you how to research, structure, write, present and produce your material in book form. Whether it's for yourself or for a wider audience, the result will be hugely satisfying. Michael Oke is a biographer and director of Bound Biographies Limited, a company which helps people write their own life story. He also gives talks and radio interviews and also leads workshops and writes articles on the subject.

144 pages. 1 85703 695 6

WRITING SHORT STORIES AND ARTICLES
How to get your work into magazines and newspapers

Adèle Ramet

Find out what really makes the difference to getting your work published in magazines and newspapers. 'Everything the beginner needs to know, but it's just as helpful for experienced writers, who will pick up all sorts of useful hints from it.' *Alison Chisholm, BBC Radio.*

152 pages. 1 85703 740 5. 2nd edition.

WRITE & SELL YOUR NOVEL
The fiction writer's guide to writing for publication

Marina Oliver

This handbook shows you how to create compelling characters, plots and subplots, and whose viewpoint to tell your story from. There are tips on how to prepare your work for submission, who to send it to and an overview of the whole publishing process. Marina Oliver has published over 30 novels, and lectures widely on writing.

157 pages. 1 85703 575 5. 2nd edition.

THE INTERNET GUIDE FOR WRITERS
How to use the internet for writing, research and information
Malcolm Chisholm

The internet is the largest source of information in the world –
universities, companies, governments, professional and
enthusiastic amateurs all contribute their knowledge. This
invaluable handbook will make sure that writers save time on
research and spend more time on writing. Malcolm Chisholm
has worked in IT for over 30 years. He runs courses for
writers on how to use IT and the Internet.

144 pages. 1 85703 715 4

WRITING FOR PUBLICATION
What to write; how to write it; where and how to sell it
Chriss McCallum

Absorbing and highly informative, this is the fourth edition of
Chriss McCallum's essential handbook. No author seriously
interested in getting published can afford to be without it.
'Really definitive . . . Leaves every other similar book in its
shade.' Pause, National Poetry Foundation.

192 pages. 1 85703 226 8. 4th edition

Made in the USA
San Bernardino, CA
12 December 2018